four ingredient
fuss-free recipes

four ingredient fuss-free recipes

OVER SIXTY SENSATIONALLY SIMPLE RECIPES USING JUST FOUR INGREDIENTS OR FEWER, SHOWN IN OVER 300 PHOTOGRAPHS

JOANNA FARROW

HERMES HOUSE

This edition is published by Hermes House
an imprint of Anness Publishing Ltd
Hermes House, 88–89 Blackfriars Road, London SE1 8HA
tel. 020 7401 2077; fax 020 7633 9499

www.hermeshouse.com; www.annesspublishing.com

Publisher: Joanna Lorenz
Editorial Director: Judith Simons
Senior Editor: Susannah Blake
Photography: Tim Auty, Martin Brigdale, Nicky Dowey, Gus Filgate, Michelle Garrett, Amanda Heywood, William Lingwood, Craig Robertson, Simon Smith
Recipes: Pepita Aris, Alex Barker, Jacqueline Clark, Joanna Farrow, Brian Glover, Jane Milton, Jennie Shapter, Marlena Spieler, Kate Whiteman
Editorial Reader: Lindsay Zamponi
Production Controller: Claire Rae

A CIP catalogue record for this book is available from the British Library.

Previously published as *Fuss-Free Food with Four Ingredients*

ETHICAL TRADING POLICY

At Anness Publishing we believe that business should be conducted in an ethical and ecologically sustainable way, with respect for the environment and a proper regard to the replacement of the natural resources we employ.

As a publisher, we use a lot of wood pulp in high-quality paper for printing, and that wood commonly comes from spruce trees. We are therefore currently growing more than 750,000 trees in three Scottish forest plantations: Berrymoss (130 hectares/320 acres), West Touxhill (125 hectares/305 acres) and Deveron Forest (75 hectares/185 acres). The forests we manage contain more than 3.5 times the number of trees employed each year in making paper for the books we manufacture.

Because of this ongoing ecological investment programme, you, as our customer, can have the pleasure and reassurance of knowing that a tree is being cultivated on your behalf to naturally replace the materials used to make the book you are holding.

Our forestry programme is run in accordance with the UK Woodland Assurance Scheme (UKWAS) and will be certified by the internationally recognized Forest Stewardship Council (FSC). The FSC is a non-government organization dedicated to promoting responsible management of the world's forests. Certification ensures forests are managed in an environmentally sustainable and socially responsible way.

For further information about this scheme, go to www.annesspublishing.com/trees

NOTES

Bracketed terms are intended for American readers.

For all recipes, quantities are given in both metric and imperial measures and, where appropriate, in standard cups and spoons.

Follow one set of measures, but not a mixture, because they are not interchangeable.

Standard spoon and cup measures are level. 1 tsp = 5ml, 1 tbsp = 15ml, 1 cup = 250ml/8fl oz.

Australian standard tablespoons are 20ml. Australian readers should use 3 tsp in place of 1 tbsp for measuring small quantities.

American pints are 16fl oz/2 cups. American readers should use 20fl oz/2.5 cups in place of 1 pint when measuring liquids.

Electric oven temperatures in this book are for conventional ovens. When using a fan oven, the temperature will probably need to be reduced by about 10–20°C/20–40°F. Since ovens vary, you should check with your manufacturer's instruction book for guidance.

Medium (US large) eggs are used unless otherwise stated.

Main front cover image shows cod with Fresh Tomato Sauce – for sauce recipe, see page 12.

PUBLISHER'S NOTE

Contents

The Minimalist Approach

In recent years, cooking and eating trends have changed considerably, with more emphasis on dishes that are quick and easy to prepare, yet that are still exciting, sophisticated and delicious. This book teaches you how to really make the most of food – with simple, fabulous recipes that use only four ingredients, or less. Using a limited number of top-quality ingredients allows you to really savour the aroma, taste and texture of a dish and saves time on writing lists and shopping for ingredients. It also allows for fuss-free preparation, giving you more time to sit back, relax and enjoy.

When you're cooking with four ingredients, each one has to be a star player. It is important to buy the best quality ingredients you can find so be selective when buying, as the better the raw materials, the more flavour the finished dish will have. Top-quality produce will also need fewer additional seasonings or flavourings to make them taste fabulous. Buying the best does not necessarily mean paying more. For example meat from a good, traditional-style butcher is often cheaper than the better-quality types in the supermarket and it will probably have a fuller flavour. Good fish can be slightly harder to find. Be particularly choosy when buying from supermarket fish counters: avoid tired-looking specimens and remember that it is better to go for good-quality frozen fish and shellfish rather than poor-quality fresh. Farmers' market stores can be great sources of good-quality fruit and vegetables, often at a good price, even for the more exotic produce.

Ready-made stocks and sauces are infinitely useful for creating quick and easy meals and are a great way to cut down on preparation and cooking time. A basic tomato sauce can lay the foundations for hundreds of different dishes such as stews, casseroles and pasta dishes. Simply add poultry, meat, fish, vegetables or pulses and flavour with fresh herbs and spices. Sauces such as pesto are great for adding flavour, while a really great ready-made custard can be the perfect base for an ice cream. Good-quality bought sauces are readily available fresh or in jars – check out the list of ingredients on the pack for some indication of the quality. A good bought liquid concentrate or fresh stock is worth keeping in the refrigerator or freezer. Remember that many bought chilled fresh products are suitable for home freezing, which is a good way of extending their shelf life. Alternatively, you can make your own supply of basic stocks and sauces and freeze them in practical, ready-to-use batches.

Choosing really fresh, good-quality ingredients will help you to create delicious, flavoursome dishes.

Fresh herbs go perfectly with other simple flavours and play an essential role in minimalist cooking.

Adding a splash of robust wine or herb-infused vinegar to a sauce or stew can help to give extra body and flavour.

Storecupboard essentials

Try to avoid overstocking the storecupboard (pantry). Choose good-quality extra-virgin olive oil and balsamic vinegar for dressings and a lighter oil such as sunflower oil for cooking. A nut oil such as walnut or hazelnut is an interesting alternative to olive oil in salad dressings. One or two flavoured oils are great for adding extra taste.

Preserved or dried vegetables such as sun-dried tomatoes, bottled roasted (bell) peppers and capers have a powerful taste and can be useful for boosting flavour in many Mediterranean-style dishes. Dried mushrooms bring a full flavour to mushroom dishes and can be good for perking up simple soups, stews, casseroles and risottos.

Keep herb and spice supplies to a minimum as both lose their flavour comparatively quickly, particularly if exposed to light and warmth. If possible, it is better to grow or buy fresh herbs and freeze any leftovers for future use rather than stocking a cupboard full of dried spices that have an inferior flavour. If possible, stock whole spices such as cumin and coriander and grind them using a mortar and pestle or in a spice grinder as required as ground spices tend to lose their flavour quickly. Freshly grated whole nutmeg is better than ready ground and it adds interest to potato dishes and white sauces.

Other essential storecupboard ingredients include salt and ground black pepper, sugar, plain (all-purpose) flour and cornflour (cornstarch), plus basic staples such as pasta and rice. It is also handy to have a small selection of condiments or sauces such as soy sauce or pesto that can help to perk up or enhance the flavour of simple dishes.

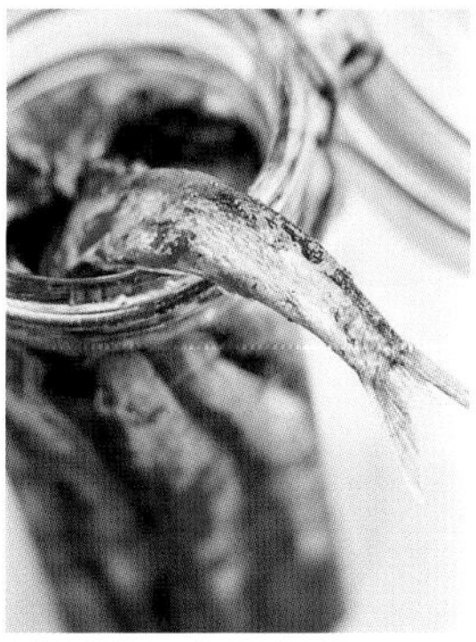

Rich-tasting anchovies are a perfect ingredient to keep in the storecupboard.

Using the recipes

Each recipe uses no more than four ingredients, excluding salt, pepper and water. Some recipes use ready-made stock or sauce – but you can always use a homemade one if you prefer. Serving suggestions and ideas for garnishes or decorations are included where appropriate, but these are not essential for the success of the dish. There are also suggestions for variations that offer alternative or additional flavourings and handy cook's tips that will help you achieve successful results every time.

Equipment

Having the right equipment makes cooking both easier and more enjoyable; chopping ingredients with a blunt knife simply becomes laborious. There are only a few items of really vital equipment. Knives, pans, mixing bowls, wooden spoons, roasting and baking tins (pans), measuring jugs (pitchers), whisks and sieves (strainers) are all essential and the following are some items to which it is worth paying special attention. Many so-called labour-saving gadgets are, more often than not, used once or twice and then put away, cluttering up storage space.

Knives

Always buy good-quality knives. Although they are quite expensive, they will last for years, so buy them as you can afford them to build up a small set. Store knives in a knife rack or wallet for safety and to protect the blades. Blades should be sharpened frequently for good performance.

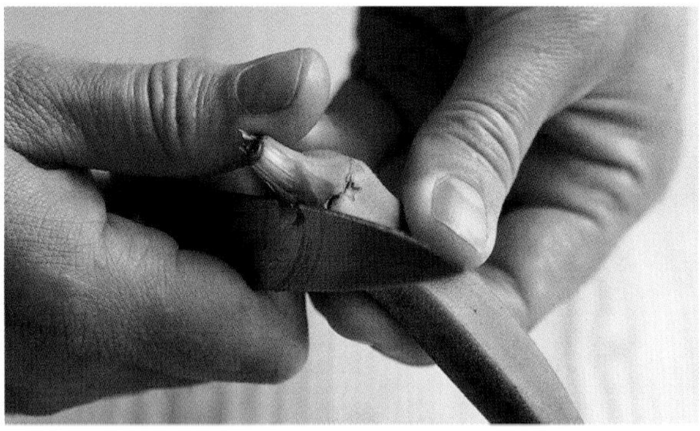

A good-quality knife is essential for preparing ingredients.

Chopping board

When chopping meat or fish, always use a plastic board and scrub well after use. However, a large, heavy sturdy wooden board is a good choice for preparing vegetables and fruit as it will not slip while in use. Avoid glass boards as they blunt knives very quickly.

Pans

Three or four different-sized pans are ample for most households. Choose heavy pans as they do not burn easily when making sauces and long-simmered dishes.

Frying pans

One large, heavy stainless steel frying pan, preferably with a lid, is sufficient in most kitchens. However, a non-stick pan is essential for dry-frying foods or for cooking in a very small amount of oil.

Wok

Even if you do not do much stir-frying or Asian-style cooking, a wok is useful for a variety of other cooking methods such as cooking and tossing pasta dishes, vegetables, tomato sauces and any other ingredients that might normally spill out of a traditional frying pan.

Weighing scales

These are useful if you make breads, cakes or any dishes requiring accurate quantities for success. There are a wide variety of different scales available from spring and balance scales to digital scales, which can be extremely accurate.

Measuring spoons

A set of metal measuring spoons is essential as table cutlery can vary widely in volume, making spoons intended for eating or serving food unsuitable for measuring quantities.

A set of measuring spoons is a small, worthwhile investment.

Measuring jugs and cups

Heatproof jugs (pitchers) marked with metric and imperial measurements are useful for measuring liquids. Cups, which vary in size from ¼–1 cup, are used in several countries to measure wet and dry ingredients.

A goblet blender is perfect for making drinks and soups.

Electrical equipment

Food processors are the most useful of all the electrical appliances, as they take the effort out of chopping, blending, grating and making pastes and purées. Some large food processors have smaller containers that fit inside the large bowl for processing smaller quantities. A blender wand or hand-held blender that processes ingredients in a pan is especially useful and, like a goblet blender, it reduces soups to a finer texture than a food processor. An electric whisk is practical for whipping cream, whisking egg whites and creaming cakes.

Cooking techniques

Allowing onions to brown caramelizes their surface and adds flavour to the final dish.

When using a limited number of ingredients, straightforward, flavour-enhancing cooking methods are the best choice. Frying, grilling (broiling) and roasting can help to enrich the ingredients, causing caramelization and browning on the surface. The cooked food will be well flavoured, needing little more than lemon wedges or a simple condiment to complete the dish. Steaming is quite different – highlighting the natural flavour of ingredients. Minimum seasonings are necessary but subtle sauces can enhance the plain cooked foods. Concentrating on simple cooking methods helps to keep the core recipe quick and easy.

Frying

This is good for enriching the natural flavour of ingredients. There are several methods: deep-frying, pan-frying or shallow-frying, stir-frying and dry-frying. Each one uses different quantities of fat and produces different results.

The initial frying of ingredients can help to determine the final character of a dish. Heat the oil before adding the ingredients and do not add too much to the pan at once. Overfilling the pan will steam or braise, rather than fry, the food, which will affect the final flavour. If necessary, fry ingredients in batches.

Stir-frying uses less oil than traditional frying methods and combines all the ingredients in one pan, bringing together a few complementary flavours. The juices yielded in stir-frying are usually sufficient to form a sauce. Dry-frying in a non-stick pan requires no fat so is ideal when trying to reduce the number of cooking ingredients.

Deep-frying can bring out rich flavours in simple ingredients.

Grilling

Cooking under a grill (broiler) or on a griddle can really bring out the flavour of good quality ingredients, imparting a rich, smoky flavour. Meat, poultry, fish, shellfish and vegetables need little more than light seasoning and brushing with oil. Time permitting, the food can be marinated in advance in a bought marinade or simple mixture of lemon juice or wine, garlic and herbs. Preheat the grill before cooking the food and baste non-fatty foods with oil, marinade or a basting mixture during grilling to prevent them from drying out.

Cooking on a griddle is quick and easy and produces delicious, attractive results.

Roasting

Traditionally a method used for cooking meat and poultry, roasting is also excellent for large pieces of fish and vegetables. The ingredients are cooked uncovered to encourage browning and the formation of a crisp and golden surface. When temperature and timing are correct the foods stay moist and succulent inside. Basting with butter or olive oil, or juices that seep out during cooking, helps to flavour and crisp the skin as well as keep the food moist.

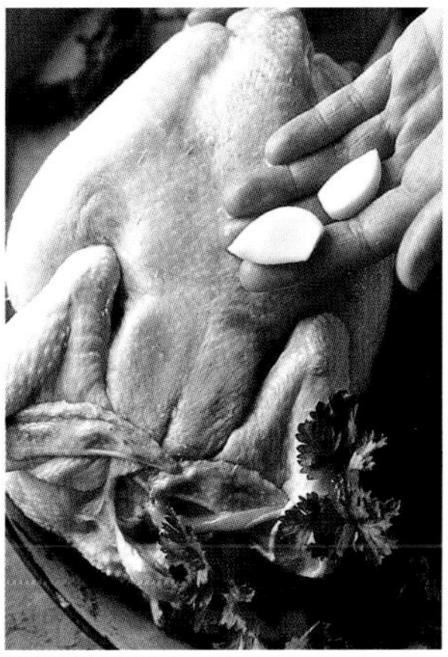

Chicken is delicious roasted with simple aromatic flavours such as garlic and herbs.

Steaming

This simple cooking method focuses on the natural, raw, taste of the food. Cooking in steam does not impart flavour in the way that frying, grilling (broiling) and roasting can so it is best used for cooking ingredients that have an excellent natural flavour, which can be savoured plain or served with an interesting sauce or accompaniment. Steaming is a gentle method that produces wonderfully moist results and is perfectly suited to vegetables and fish. Check food frequently during steaming as some foods cook surprisingly quickly.

Making Basic Stocks

A well-flavoured stock is particularly good in dishes that rely on minimal ingredients. Good-quality ready-made stocks – either cube, powders or liquid concentrate – are readily available but stocks are easy and cheap to make. Always ask for the meat bones when buying from a butcher and trimmings if you have fish prepared by the fishmonger as these are perfect for making good stock. A chicken carcass from a roast makes excellent stock, particularly if you've packed it with herbs, onions, garlic or other aromatics before roasting. A good vegetable stock can be made from trimmings when preparing vegetables and small quantities of leftover produce. Leave the onion skins on if you want a rich, dark-coloured stock.

Beef Stock MAKES ABOUT 1 LITRE/1¾ PINTS/4 CUPS

900g/2lb beef bones

2 unpeeled onions, quartered

1 bouquet garni

2 large carrots, roughly chopped

1 Preheat the oven to 220°C/425°F/Gas 7. Put the beef bones in a roasting pan and roast for about 45 minutes, or until well browned.

2 Transfer the roasted bones to a large, heavy pan. Add the onion quarters, leaving the skins on, the bouquet garni and chopped carrots. Add 5ml/1 tsp salt and 5ml/1 tsp black peppercorns. Pour over about 1.7 litres/3 pints/7½ cups cold water and bring just to the boil.

3 Using a slotted spoon, skim off any scum on the surface of the stock. Reduce the heat and partially cover the pan. Simmer the stock on the lowest heat for about 3 hours, then set aside to cool slightly.

4 Strain the stock into a large bowl and leave to cool completely, then remove any fat from the surface. Store the stock in the refrigerator for up to 3 days or freeze for up to 6 months.

Chicken Stock MAKES ABOUT 1 LITRE/1¾ PINTS/4 CUPS

1 large roast chicken carcass

2 unpeeled onions, quartered

3 bay leaves

2 large carrots, roughly chopped

1 Put the chicken carcass and any loose bones and roasting juices into a heavy pan in which they fit snugly. Add the onion quarters, bay leaves and chopped carrots.

2 Add 2.5ml/½ tsp salt and 5ml/1 tsp black peppercorns to the pan, and pour over 1.7 litres/3 pints/7½ cups cold water. Bring just to the boil.

3 Reduce the heat, partially cover the pan and cook on the lowest setting for about 1½ hours. Using a large spoon, carefully turn the chicken in the stock and crush the carcass occasionally.

4 Leave the stock to cool slightly, then strain into a large bowl and leave to cool completely. When cool, remove any fat from the surface. Store the stock in the refrigerator for up to 2 days or freeze for up to 6 months.

Fish Stock MAKES ABOUT 600ML/1 PINT/2½ CUPS

500g/1¼ lb fish bones and trimmings, without heads and gills

1 bouquet garni

1 onion or 3–4 shallots, peeled and quartered

2 celery sticks, roughly chopped

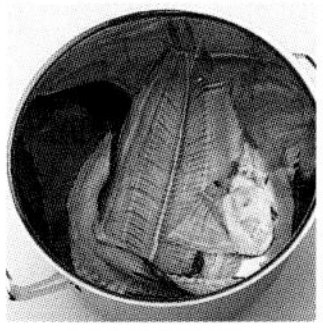

1 Pack the fish bones and trimmings into a heavy pan and add the bouquet garni, quartered onion or shallots and celery.

2 Add 2.5ml/½ tsp salt and 2.5ml/½ tsp peppercorns to the pan and pour over 1 litre/1¾ pints/4 cups water. Bring to the boil.

3 Reduce the heat, partially cover the pan and cook on the lowest setting for about 30 minutes, stirring occasionally. Leave to cool slightly, then strain into a bowl and cool completely. Store in the refrigerator for up to 24 hours or freeze for up to 3 months.

Vegetable Stock MAKES ABOUT 1 LITRE/1¾ PINTS/4 CUPS

3 unpeeled onions, quartered

200g/7oz large open mushrooms

300–400g/11–14oz mixed vegetables, such as broccoli, carrots, celery, tomatoes and/or spring onions (scallions), roughly chopped

45ml/3 tbsp green or brown lentils

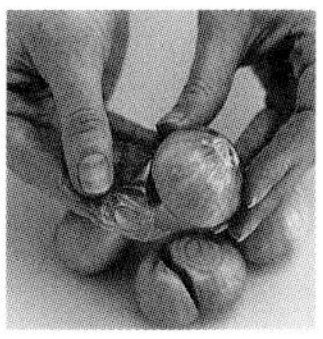

1 Place the onions in a heavy pan with the mushrooms, mixed vegetables and green or brown lentils.

2 Add 2.5ml/½ tsp salt, 10ml/2 tsp peppercorns and 1.7 litres/3 pints/7½ cups water to the pan. Bring to the boil, then reduce the heat and simmer, partially covered, for 50–60 minutes.

3 Leave the stock to cool slightly, then strain into a bowl and leave to cool. Store in the refrigerator for up to 24 hours or freeze for up to 6 months.

Bouquet Garni

This little bundle of herbs is perfect for adding flavour to stocks, soups and stews. Tying the herbs in a bundle means that the bouquet garni is easy to remove after cooking. A traditional bouquet garni comprises sprigs of parsley, thyme and a bay leaf, but you can vary the herbs according to the dish and/or main ingredients. Rosemary and oregano are good with lamb, while mint, chervil, basil, chives and tarragon go well with fish.

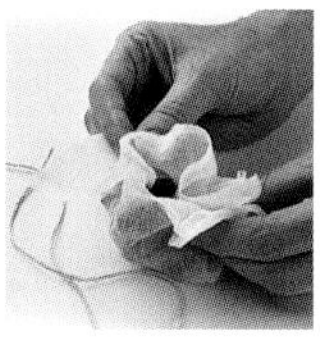

1 Using a short length of string, tie together a bay leaf and sprigs of thyme and parsley.

2 Alternatively, place the herbs in the centre of a square of muslin (cheesecloth) and tie into a neat bundle using a short length of string.

3 Use the bouquet garni immediately or freeze, ready for cooking. (Herbs tied in muslin are better suited to freezing than bundles simply tied with string.)

FREEZING STOCK

The main ingredients for stock can be frozen – meat bones, fish trimmings or a cooked chicken carcass – ready to make home-made stock at a later date.

More conveniently, stock itself freezes very well. Once the stock has been strained and the fat removed, reduce the volume by boiling the stock uncovered. This concentrates its flavour and takes up less freezer space. A highly reduced stock, boiled to a thick syrup, can be frozen in an ice cube tray. Make a note of the volume before boiling, then add this to the label when packing the stock for the freezer. This way you will know how much water to add when the concentrated stock is thawed.

Making Basic Savoury Sauces

A good sauce can provide the finishing touch for a dish. There are a large number of ready-made sauces available, but they are also very easy to make yourself. One of the most basic sauces is the classic savoury white sauce, which can be served as a simple topping for vegetables or flavoured with additional ingredients such as cheese, herbs, onions or mushrooms and served with pasta, fish or poultry. A basic fresh tomato sauce is widely used for pasta dishes, pizza toppings and vegetable dishes and it is worth making when ripe tomatoes are available. It can be stored in the refrigerator for several days or can be frozen for up to 6 months. Hollandaise sauce is another classic accompaniment for fish and vegetables. Unlike the other sauces it cannot be made ahead, but it is available commercially.

White Sauce MAKES ABOUT 300ML/½ PINT/1¼ CUPS

300ml/½ pint/1¼ cups milk

15g/½oz/1 tbsp butter

15g/½oz plain (all-purpose) flour

freshly grated nutmeg

1 Warm the milk in a small pan. In a separate pan, melt the butter over a gentle heat, then add the flour and cook, stirring, for 1 minute until the mixture forms a thick paste.

2 Remove the pan from the heat and gradually add the warmed milk, whisking continuously until smooth.

3 Return the pan to a gentle heat and cook, whisking, until the sauce boils, is smooth and thickened. Season with salt and freshly ground pepper and plenty of nutmeg.

Fresh Tomato Sauce MAKES ABOUT 1 LITRE/1¾ PINTS/4 CUPS

1.3kg/3lb ripe tomatoes

120ml/4fl oz/½ cup garlic-infused (-steeped) olive oil

1 large onion, finely chopped

small handful of basil leaves, torn, or 30ml/2 tbsp chopped fresh oregano

1 Put the tomatoes in a bowl, pour over boiling water to cover and leave to stand for about 1 minute until the skins split. Drain and peel, then roughly chop the flesh.

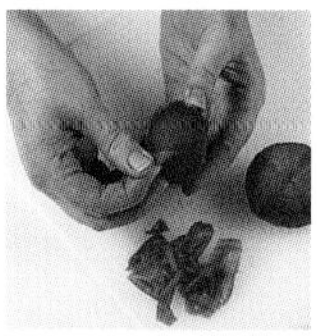

2 Heat half the oil in a large heavy pan. Add the chopped onion and cook gently for about 3 minutes, or until softened but not browned.

3 Add the tomatoes and the remaining oil to the pan and cook gently, stirring, for 5 minutes, or until the tomatoes are soft and juicy.

4 Add the herbs, cover and cook gently for 20–25 minutes, stirring frequently, until the sauce is thickened and pulpy. Season to taste.

VARIATIONS

- *Try using different herbs such as flat leaf parsley, marjoram, thyme, rosemary or coriander (cilantro) in place of the basil or oregano.*
- *To make a warm, mildly peppery sauce add a little paprika, or to make a spicy sauce, add a little chilli powder (or a finely chopped fresh chilli).*
- *To make a much more garlicky sauce, add 2–3 crushed garlic cloves to the pan just before adding the chopped tomatoes.*

Hollandaise Sauce MAKES ABOUT 120ML/4FL OZ/½ CUP

45ml/3 tbsp white wine or herb-infused vinegar

1 bay leaf

2 egg yolks

115g/4oz/½ cup butter, chilled

COOK'S TIP *The sauce can be kept warm in a covered bowl set over the pan of hot water for up to 20 minutes. If the sauce is very thick, whisk in a few drops of hot water. If the sauce starts to separate, whisk in an ice cube.*

1 Put the vinegar in a small pan with the bay leaf and add 5ml/1 tsp black peppercorns. Boil rapidly until reduced to 15ml/1 tbsp, then strain into a heatproof bowl.

2 Put the vinegar in a clean pan, add the egg yolks and a little salt and whisk lightly until thoroughly combined. Cut the chilled butter into small pieces.

3 Add the butter to the pan and set the pan over a very low heat. Whisk continuously so that as the butter melts it is blended into the egg yolks. When all the butter has melted, continue whisking until the sauce is thick and smooth.

4 Season the sauce with salt and ground black pepper to taste, adding a few extra drops of vinegar, if you like, to give a slightly tangy flavour. Serve warm.

Mayonnaise MAKES 150ML/¼ PINT/⅔ CUP

1 egg yolk, at room temperature

15ml/1 tbsp lemon juice or white wine vinegar

5ml/1 tsp Dijon mustard

150ml/¼ pint/⅔ cup olive oil

1 Put the egg yolk in a bowl with the lemon juice or vinegar, mustard and a little salt. Whisk together until combined.

2 Gradually add the oil in a thin trickle, whisking continuously until the sauce is thickened and smooth. This will take several minutes.

3 Check the seasoning, adding a few drops of lemon juice or vinegar if the mayonnaise is too bland. If the sauce is too thick, stir in a few drops of warm water. Cover with clear film (plastic wrap) and store in the refrigerator for up to 2 days.

Flavoured Oils

There are plenty of flavoured oils available in delicatessens and supermarkets, infused (steeped) with aromatics such as lemon, garlic, herbs and chillies, which are delicious served as a simple dressing for freshly cooked pasta or a salad. Home-made versions are less expensive and you can be more selective with the flavours you choose. Once made, the oil should be left in a cool place for up to a week to allow the flavours to infuse. Then the oil should be strained before storing. The aromatic ingredients should not be stored long term in the oil, because of the risk of harmful moulds developing.

Basil Oil Blend a large handful of basil leaves with 200ml/7fl oz/scant 1 cup olive oil in a food processor. Leave overnight, then strain through a muslin- (cheesecloth-) lined sieve (strainer) into a clean bowl. Store in the refrigerator, then bring to room temperature before using.

Garlic and Rosemary Oil Put a handful of rosemary sprigs in a pan with 3 sliced garlic cloves and 120ml/4fl oz/½ cup olive oil. Heat gently until bubbling, then pour into a heatproof bowl, cover and leave in a cool place overnight. Strain the garlic and rosemary oil into a clean 300–400ml/10–14fl oz/1¼–1⅔ cup bottle and top up with more oil.

Making Basic Sweet Sauces

From creamy, comforting custard to an elegant fruit coulis, sweet sauces can be used to uplift the simplest puddings and desserts to create a truly spectacular dish. They can be served as an accompaniment or make up an intrinsic part of a dish. Simple vanilla ice cream is taken to new levels when served with hot chocolate sauce or a fresh raspberry coulis, while a classic vanilla custard can be used as the base of a sweet soufflé. These sweet sauces rely on just a few basic ingredients and minimal effort, producing irresistible results. The dessert sauce can be made in advance, before serving the meal, ready for reheating or serving cold. Even custard can be re-heated, just take care to use very gentle heat to prevent it from curdling.

Real Custard MAKES 300ML/½ PINT/1¼ CUPS

300ml/½ pint/1¼ cups full-cream (whole) milk or half milk and half double (heavy) cream

3 egg yolks

5ml/1 tsp cornflour (cornstarch)

45ml/3 tbsp caster (superfine) sugar or vanilla sugar

1 Pour the milk or milk and cream mixture into a double boiler or heavy pan and bring slowly to the boil over a very gentle heat.

2 Meanwhile, whisk the egg yolks with the cornflour and sugar until thoroughly mixed. Pour the boiled milk into the yolk mixture, whisking continuously until combined.

3 Pour the mixture back into the cleaned pan and cook over the lowest heat, stirring continuously with a wooden spoon, for 8–10 minutes, or until the mixture coats the back of the spoon.

4 Immediately pour the custard through a sieve (strainer) into a bowl or jug (pitcher) to prevent it from overcooking. Serve warm.

COOK'S TIP

Always cook custard over the lowest heat possible to reduce the risk of curdling. Adding a little cornflour to the sauce helps to prevent it from curdling without affecting the consistency or flavour.

Summer Fruit Coulis MAKES ABOUT 250ML/8FL OZ/1 CUP

130g/4½oz raspberries

130g/4½oz strawberries

10–15ml/2–3 tsp icing (confectioners') sugar

15ml/1 tbsp orange liqueur or Kirsch (optional)

1 Place the raspberries and strawberries in a food processor and process until smooth. Press the mixture through a fine strainer set over a bowl to remove the tiny seeds.

2 Return the strained fruit purée to the food processor or blender and add 10ml/2 tsp of the icing sugar with the orange liqueur or kirsch, if using, and process briefly until well combined.

3 Check the sweetness of the coulis, then add a little more icing sugar if necessary and process again to mix.

Rich Chocolate Sauce MAKES ABOUT 250ML/8FL OZ/1 CUP

130g/4½oz caster (superfine) sugar

175g/6oz plain (semisweet) chocolate, broken into pieces

25g/1oz/2 tbsp unsalted (sweet) butter

30ml/2 tbsp brandy or coffee liqueur (optional)

1 Put the sugar in a small heavy pan with 120ml/4fl oz/½ cup water and heat gently until the sugar dissolves. Bring to the boil and boil for 1 minute.

2 Remove from the heat and stir in the chocolate and butter, stirring until the chocolate has melted and the sauce is smooth.

3 Stir in the brandy or coffee liqueur, if using, and serve warm.

Rosemary and Almond Cream MAKES ABOUT 600ML/1 PINT/2½ CUPS

This deliciously fragrant cream is more of an accompaniment than a sauce and is an excellent alternative to plain whipped cream served with fruit compotes, pies and tarts or a bowl of fresh fruits. Rosemary works really well (particularly if you then decorate the dish with flowering sprigs) but bay leaves or thyme sprigs also provide a lovely flavour.

300ml/½ pint/1¼ cups double (heavy) cream

2 rosemary sprigs

25g/1oz/½ cup finely ground amaretti or macaroon biscuits

15ml/1 tbsp almond liqueur such as amaretto (optional)

1 Pour the double cream into a pan, then add the rosemary sprigs and heat gently until the cream bubbles. Leave the mixture to cool, then strain into a bowl.

2 Add the finely ground biscuits to the flavoured cream and add 15ml/1 tbsp almond liqueur, if you like.

3 Whisk the cream and crushed biscuits together until the mixture is just holding its shape, then transfer to a serving dish and chill until ready to serve.

Flavoured Sugar

A store of herb- and spice-infused (-steeped) sugars provides plenty of flavouring options for sauces, desserts and cakes without the need for additional ingredients. Vanilla sugar is the best known and can be bought easily, but there are many other equally useful flavours. Use in any recipe instead of ordinary sugar or use half flavoured and half ordinary sugar.

Vanilla Sugar Half fill a small jar with white or golden caster (superfine) sugar and add 1 vanilla pod (bean). Top up with sugar, seal and store in a cool place for a week before using.

Spice Sugar Half fill a small jar with caster (superfine) sugar and add either 2 broken cinnamon sticks, 15ml/1 tbsp lightly bruised cardamom pods, or 4 star anise and top up with more sugar. Seal and store in a cool dark place for about a week before using.

Flower or Herb Sugar Half fill a small jar with caster (superfine) sugar and add either a handful of fresh, dry rose petals; several sprigs of lavender, rosemary or thyme; or several bay leaves. Shake gently to distribute the flowers or herbs and top up with more sugar, seal and store in a cool dark place for about a week before using.

Soups and Appetizers

THIS CHAPTER IS PACKED WITH FABULOUS IDEAS FOR QUICK AND SIMPLE SOUPS AND APPETIZERS THAT CAN MAKE A DELICIOUS MEAL EVEN MORE SPECIAL. EACH RECIPE USES JUST FOUR INGREDIENTS AND TASTES SENSATIONAL, AND THERE ARE EVEN HANDY TIPS AND SUGGESTIONS ON HOW TO VARY THE FLAVOURS AND INGREDIENTS. TRY SIMPLE SNACKS SUCH AS CREAM OF ONION SOUP, OR MORE SOPHISTICATED DISHES SUCH AS RED ONION AND GOAT'S CHEESE PASTRIES.

Simple Cream of Onion Soup

This wonderfully soothing soup has a deep, buttery flavour that is achieved with only a few ingredients and the minimum of fuss. It makes delicious comfort food on a cold day. Use home-made stock if you have it, or buy fresh stock for the best flavour. Crisp croûtons or chopped chives complement the smooth soup when sprinkled over just before serving.

SERVES FOUR

115g/4oz/ ½ cup unsalted (sweet) butter

1kg/2¼lb yellow onions, sliced

1 litre/1¾ pints/4 cups good chicken or vegetable stock

150ml/¼ pint/⅔ cup double (heavy) cream

COOK'S TIP

Adding the second batch of onions gives texture and a lovely buttery flavour to this soup. Make sure the onions do not brown or crisp.

1 Melt 75g/3oz/6 tbsp of the unsalted butter in a large, heavy pan. Set about 200g/7oz of the onions aside and add the rest to the pan. Stir to coat in the butter, then cover and cook very gently for about 30 minutes. The onions should be very soft and tender, but not browned.

2 Add the chicken or vegetable stock, 5ml/1 tsp salt and freshly ground black pepper to taste. Bring to the boil, reduce the heat and simmer for 5 minutes, then remove from the heat.

3 Leave the soup to cool, then process it in a blender or food processor. Return the soup to the rinsed pan.

4 Meanwhile, melt the remaining butter in another pan and cook the remaining onions over a low heat, covered, until soft but not browned. Uncover and continue to cook the onions gently until they turn golden yellow.

5 Add the cream to the soup and reheat it gently until hot, but do not allow it to boil. Taste and adjust the seasoning. Add the buttery onions and stir for 1–2 minutes, then ladle the soup into bowls. Serve the soup immediately.

Potato and Roasted Garlic Broth

Roasted garlic takes on a mellow, sweet flavour that is subtle, not overpowering, in this delicious vegetarian soup. Choose floury potatoes for this soup, such as Maris Piper, Estima, Cara or King Edward – they will give the soup a delicious velvety texture. Serve the broth piping hot with melted Cheddar or Gruyère cheese on French bread, as the perfect winter warmer.

SERVES FOUR

2 small or 1 large whole head of garlic (about 20 cloves)

4 medium potatoes (about 500g/1¼lb in total), diced

1.75 litres/3 pints/7½ cups good-quality hot vegetable stock

chopped flat leaf parsley, to garnish

1 Preheat the oven to 190°C/375°F/Gas 5. Place the unpeeled garlic bulbs or bulb in a small roasting pan and bake for 30 minutes until soft in the centre.

2 Meanwhile, par-boil the potatoes in a large pan of lightly salted boiling water for 10 minutes.

3 Simmer the stock in another pan for 5 minutes. Drain the potatoes and add them to the stock.

4 Squeeze the garlic pulp into the soup, reserving a few whole cloves, stir and season to taste. Simmer for 15 minutes and serve topped with whole garlic cloves and parsley.

Winter Squash Soup with Tomato Salsa

Creamy butternut squash makes good soup with very few additional ingredients. Select a really good bought salsa for this soup and add a sprinkling of chopped fresh oregano or marjoram as a garnish.

SERVES FOUR TO FIVE

1 large butternut squash or small pumpkin, halved and seeded

75ml/5 tbsp garlic-flavoured olive oil

2 onions, chopped

60–120ml/4–8 tbsp tomato salsa

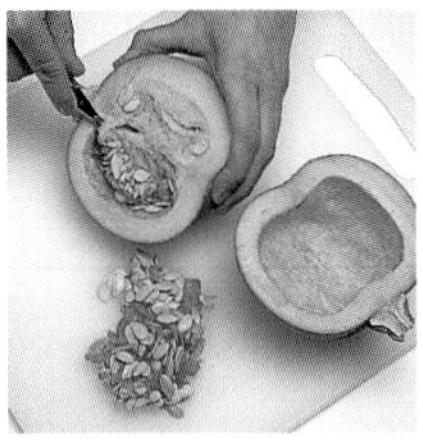

1 Preheat the oven to 220°C/425°F/Gas 7. Place the butternut squash or pumpkin on a baking sheet and brush with some of the oil and roast for 25 minutes. Reduce the temperature to 190°C/375°F/Gas 5 and cook for 20–25 minutes more, or until the squash is tender.

2 Heat the remaining oil in a large, heavy pan and cook the chopped onions over a low heat for about 10 minutes, or until softened.

3 Meanwhile, scoop the squash out of its skin, adding it to the pan. Pour in 1.2 litres/ 2 pints/5 cups water and stir in 5ml/1 tsp salt and plenty of black pepper. Bring to the boil, cover and simmer for 10 minutes.

4 Cool the soup slightly, then process it in a blender or food processor to a smooth purée. Alternatively, press the soup through a fine sieve with the back of a spoon. Reheat without boiling, then ladle it into warmed bowls. Top each serving with a spoonful of salsa and serve.

Vichyssoise

This classic, chilled summer soup of leeks and potatoes was first created in the 1920s by Louis Diat, chef at the New York Ritz-Carlton. He named it after Vichy near his home in France. The soup can be sharpened with lemon juice, enriched with swirls of cream and garnished with chives.

SERVES FOUR TO SIX

50g/2oz/¼ cup unsalted (sweet) butter

600g/1lb 5oz leeks, white parts only, thinly sliced

250g/9oz floury potatoes (such as King Edward or Maris Piper), peeled and cut into chunks

1.5 litres/2½ pints/6½ cups half and half light chicken stock or water and milk

1 Melt the unsalted butter in a heavy pan and cook the leeks, covered, for 15–20 minutes, until they are soft but not browned.

2 Add the potato chunks and cook over a low heat, uncovered, for a few minutes.

3 Stir in the stock or water and milk, with salt and pepper to taste. Bring to the boil, then reduce the heat and partly cover the pan. Simmer for 15 minutes, or until the potatoes are soft.

4 Cool, then process the soup until smooth in a blender or food processor. Sieve the soup into a bowl. Taste and adjust the seasoning and add a little iced water if the consistency of the soup seems too thick.

5 Chill the soup for at least 4 hours or until very cold. Taste the chilled soup for seasoning again before serving. Pour the soup into bowls and serve.

EXTRAS

To make a fabulous chilled leek and sorrel or watercress soup, add about 50g/2oz/1 cup shredded sorrel to the soup at the end of cooking. Finish and chill as in the main recipe, then serve the soup garnished with a little pile of finely shredded sorrel. The same quantity of watercress can also be used.

Sweet and Salty Vegetable Crisps

This delightfully simple snack is perfect to serve with pre-dinner drinks as an informal appetizer. Serve them with a bowl of aioli or a creamy dip such as hummus or taramasalata, and use the crisps to scoop it up. You can cook other sweet root vegetables, such as carrots and sweet potatoes, in the same way. Make a pretty, appetizing snack by making several different types of vegetable crisps, then pile them together in a bowl.

SERVES FOUR

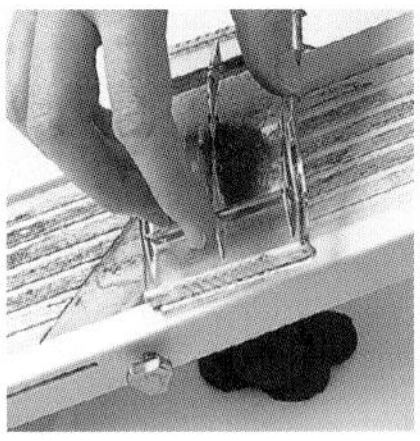

1 Peel the beetroot and, using a mandolin or a vegetable peeler, cut it into very thin slices. Lay the slices on kitchen paper and sprinkle them with sugar and fine salt.

2 Heat 5cm/2in oil in a pan, until a bread cube dropped into the pan turns golden in 1 minute. Cook the slices, in batches, until they float to the surface and turn golden at the edge. Drain on kitchen paper and sprinkle with salt when cool.

1 small fresh beetroot (beet)

caster (superfine) sugar and salt, for sprinkling

olive oil, for frying

Sizzling Prawns

These richly flavoured prawns (shrimp) are a classic Spanish tapas dish, but they also make a perfect appetizer. Traditionally they are brought to the table in little individual earthenware dishes, sizzling frantically in the hot oil with garlic. The addition of fiery chillies gives them an additional kick, but if you prefer a milder appetizer, simply omit the chillies.

SERVES FOUR

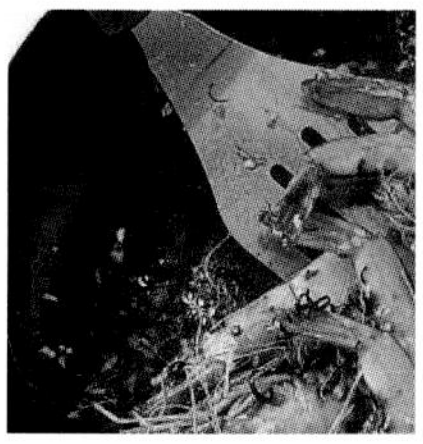

1 Split the chillies lengthways and discard the seeds. (Wash your hands with soap and water immediately.)

2 Heat the olive oil in a large frying pan and stir-fry the garlic and chillies for 1 minute, until the garlic begins to turn brown.

3 Add the whole prawns and stir-fry for 3–4 minutes, coating them well with the flavoured oil.

4 Remove the pan from the heat and divide the prawns among four dishes. Spoon over the flavoured oil and serve immediately. (Remember to provide a plate for the heads and shells, plus plenty of napkins.)

1–2 dried chillies (to taste)

60ml/4 tbsp olive oil

3 garlic cloves, finely chopped

16 large raw prawns (shrimp), in the shell

Yogurt Cheese in Olive Oil

In Greece, sheep's yogurt is hung in muslin (cheesecloth) to drain off the whey before being patted into balls of soft cheese. Here the cheese is bottled in extra virgin olive oil with dried chillies and fresh herbs to make a wonderfully aromatic first appetizer. It is delicious spread on thick slices of toast or thin wheat crackers and served as a simple yet sumptuous first course.

FILLS TWO 450G/1LB JARS

1 Sterilize a 30cm/12in square of muslin (cheesecloth) by soaking it in boiling water. Drain and lay it over a large plate. Season the yogurt generously with salt and tip on to the centre of the muslin. Bring up the sides of the muslin and tie firmly with string.

2 Hang the bag on a kitchen cupboard handle or suitable position where it can be suspended over a bowl to catch the whey. Leave for 2–3 days until the yogurt stops dripping.

3 Sterilize two 450g/1lb glass preserving or jam jars by heating them in the oven at 150°C/300°F/Gas 2 for 15 minutes.

4 Mix the crushed dried chillies and herbs. Take teaspoonfuls of the cheese and roll into balls with your hands. Lower into the jars, sprinkling each layer with the herb mixture.

5 Pour the oil over the cheese until completely covered. Store in the refrigerator for up to 3 weeks. To serve, spoon the cheese out of the jars with a little of the flavoured olive oil and spread on slices of lightly toasted bread.

1 litre/1¾ pints/ 4 cups Greek sheep's (US strained plain) yogurt

10ml/2 tsp crushed dried chillies or chilli powder

30ml/2 tbsp chopped fresh herbs, such as rosemary, and thyme or oregano

about 300ml/½ pint/ 1¼ cups extra virgin olive oil, preferably garlic-flavoured

Baked Eggs with Creamy Leeks

This simple but elegant appetizer is perfect for last-minute entertaining or quick dining. Garnish the baked eggs with crisp, fried fresh sage leaves and serve with warm, fresh crusty bread for a special meal. Small- to medium-sized leeks (less than 2.5cm/1in in diameter) are best for this dish as they have the most tender flavour and only require a short cooking time.

SERVES FOUR

15g/½oz/1 tbsp butter, plus extra for greasing

225g/8oz small leeks, thinly sliced

75–90ml/5–6 tbsp whipping cream

4 small–medium (US medium–large) eggs

1 Preheat the oven to 190°C/375°F/Gas 5. Generously butter the base and sides of four ramekins.

2 Melt the butter in a frying pan and cook the leeks over a medium heat, stirring frequently, for 3–5 minutes, until softened and translucent, but not browned.

3 Add 45ml/3 tbsp of the cream and cook over a low heat for 5 minutes, until the leeks are very soft and the cream has thickened a little. Season to taste.

4 Place the ramekins in a small roasting pan and divide the leeks among them. Break an egg into each, spoon over the remaining cream and season.

5 Pour boiling water into the roasting pan to come about halfway up the sides of the ramekins. Transfer the pan to the oven and bake in the preheated oven for about 10 minutes, until just set. Serve piping hot.

COOK'S TIP

For a slightly different result, beat the eggs with the remaining whipping cream and seasoning in step 4 and spoon over the leeks, then bake in the roasting pan as for step 5.

Potato and Onion Tortilla

This deep-set omelette with sliced potatoes and onions is the best-known Spanish tortilla and makes a deliciously simple appetizer when served with a refreshing, leafy salad. Tortilla are often made with a variety of ingredients – chopped red or yellow (bell) peppers, cooked peas, corn, or grated Cheddar or Gruyère cheese can all be added to the mixture in step 2, if you like.

SERVES FOUR TO SIX

800g/1¾lb medium potatoes

100ml/3½fl oz/ scant ½ cup extra virgin olive oil

2 onions, thinly sliced

6 eggs

1 Thinly slice the potatoes. Heat 75ml/5 tbsp of the oil in a frying pan and cook the potatoes, turning frequently, for 10 minutes. Add the onions and seasoning, and continue to cook gently for a further 10 minutes, until the vegetables are tender.

2 Meanwhile, beat the eggs in a large bowl with a little seasoning. Tip the potatoes and onions into the eggs and mix gently. Leave to stand for 10 minutes.

3 Wipe out the pan with kitchen paper and heat the remaining oil in it. Pour the egg mixture into the pan and spread it out in an even layer. Cover and cook over a very gentle heat for 20 minutes, until the eggs are just set. Serve cut into wedges.

Red Onion and Goat's Cheese Pastries

These attractive little tartlets couldn't be easier to make. Garnish them with fresh thyme sprigs and serve as a sophisticated first course for a dinner party. A wide variety of different types of goat's cheeses are available – the creamy log-shaped types without a rind are most suitable for these pastries. Ordinary onions can be used instead of red, if you prefer.

SERVES FOUR

15ml/1 tbsp olive oil

450g/1lb red onions, sliced

425g/15oz packet ready-rolled puff pastry

115g/4oz/1 cup goat's cheese, cubed

1 Heat the oil in a large, heavy frying pan, add the onions and cook over a gentle heat for 10 minutes, or until softened, stirring occasionally to prevent them from browning. Add seasoning to taste and cook for a further 2 minutes. Remove the pan from the heat and leave to cool.

2 Preheat the oven to 220°C/425°F/Gas 7. Unroll the puff pastry and using a 15cm/6in plate as a guide, cut out four rounds. Place the pastry rounds on a dampened baking sheet and, using the point of a sharp knife, score a border, 2cm/¾in inside the edge of each pastry round.

3 Divide the onions among the pastry rounds and top with the goat's cheese. Bake for 25–30 minutes until golden brown.

EXTRAS

To make richer-flavoured pastries ring the changes by spreading the pastry base with red or green pesto or tapenade before you top with the goat's cheese and cooked onions.

Pepperonata

This richly flavoured spicy tomato and sweet red pepper dip is delicious served with crisp Italian-style bread sticks – enjoy it with drinks before dinner or as a snack while watching television. It also makes a tasty relish served with grilled chicken and fish dishes. It is delicious served hot, cold or at room temperature and can be stored in the refrigerator for several days.

SERVES FOUR

1 Heat the oil in a large pan over a low heat and add the sliced peppers. Cook very gently, stirring occasionally for 3–4 minutes.

2 Add the chilli flakes to the pan and cook for 1 minute, then pour in the tomatoes and season. Cook gently for 50 minutes to 1 hour, stirring occasionally.

COOK'S TIP

Long, slow cooking helps to bring out the sweetness of the peppers and tomatoes, so don't be tempted to cheat on the cooking time by cooking over a higher heat.

2 large red (bell) peppers, halved, seeded and sliced

pinch dried chilli flakes

400g/14oz can pomodorino tomatoes

FROM THE STORECUPBOARD

60ml/4 tbsp garlic-infused olive oil

salt and ground black pepper

Artichoke and Cumin Dip

This dip is so easy to make and is unbelievably tasty. Serve with olives, hummus and wedges of pitta bread to make a summery snack selection. Grilled artichokes bottled in oil have a fabulous flavour and can be used instead of canned artichokes. You can also vary the flavourings – try adding chilli powder in place of the cumin and add a handful of basil leaves to the artichokes before blending.

SERVES FOUR

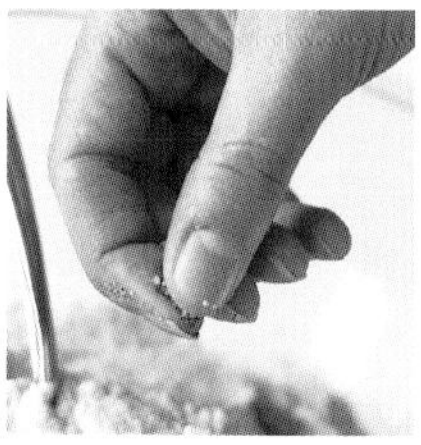

1 Put the artichoke hearts in a food processor with the garlic and ground cumin, and a generous drizzle of olive oil. Process to a smooth purée and season with plenty of salt and ground black pepper to taste.

2 Spoon the purée into a serving bowl and serve with an extra drizzle of olive oil swirled on the top and slices of warm pitta bread for dipping.

2 x 400g/14oz cans artichoke hearts, drained

2 garlic cloves, peeled

2.5ml/½ tsp ground cumin

FROM THE STORECUPBOARD

olive oil

salt and ground black pepper

Main Meals

PASTA, RICE, FRESH FISH AND GOOD QUALITY CUTS OF MEAT ALL MAKE THE PERFECT BASE FOR DELICIOUS MAIN DISHES. THE JUDICIOUS ADDITION OF FRAGRANT HERBS, PUNGENT SPICES AND OTHER WELL-FLAVOURED FRESH VEGETABLES CAN TRANSFORM THESE SIMPLE INGREDIENTS INTO TRULY MEMORABLE MEALS. TRY ROSEMARY-SCENTED LAMB STEAKS WITH REDCURRANT GLAZE OR BAKED SALMON WITH CARAWAY SEEDS AND LEMON JUICE. WHATEVER YOUR PREFERENCE, YOU ARE SURE TO FIND THE PERFECT DISH FOR ANY OCCASION.

Spaghettini with Roasted Garlic

If you have never tried roasting garlic, then this is the recipe that will convert you to its delicious mellowed sweetness. Spaghettini is very fine spaghetti, but any long thin pasta can be used in this dish – try spaghetti, linguine, tagliatelle or capellini. This simple pasta dish is very good served with a mixed leaf salad dressed with lemon juice and extra virgin olive oil.

SERVES FOUR

1 whole head of garlic

120ml/4fl oz/½ cup extra virgin olive oil

400g/14oz fresh or dried spaghettini

coarsely shaved Parmesan cheese

1 Preheat the oven to 180°C/350°F/Gas 4. Place the garlic in an oiled roasting pan and roast it for 30 minutes.

2 Leave the garlic to cool, then lay it on its side and slice off the top one-third with a sharp knife.

3 Hold the garlic over a bowl and dig out the flesh from each clove with the point of the knife. When all the flesh has been added to the bowl, pour in the oil and add plenty of black pepper. Mix well.

4 Cook the pasta in a pan of salted boiling water according to the instructions on the packet. Drain the pasta and return it to the clean pan. Pour in the oil and garlic mixture and toss the pasta vigorously over a medium heat until all the strands are thoroughly coated. Serve immediately, with shavings of Parmesan.

EXTRAS

For a fiery finish, sprinkle crushed, dried red chillies over the pasta when tossing it with the oil and garlic.

Spaghetti with Raw Tomato and Ricotta Sauce

This wonderfully simple uncooked sauce goes well with many different kinds of freshly cooked pasta, both long strands such as spaghetti, tagliatelle or linguini, and short shapes such as macaroni, rigatoni or penne. It is always at its best in summer when made with rich, sweet plum tomatoes that have ripened on the vine in the sun and have their fullest flavour.

SERVES FOUR

500g/1¼lb ripe Italian plum tomatoes

75ml/5 tbsp garlic-flavoured olive oil

350g/12oz dried spaghetti or pasta of your choice

115g/4oz ricotta salata cheese, diced

1 Coarsely chop the plum tomatoes, removing the cores and as many of the seeds as you can.

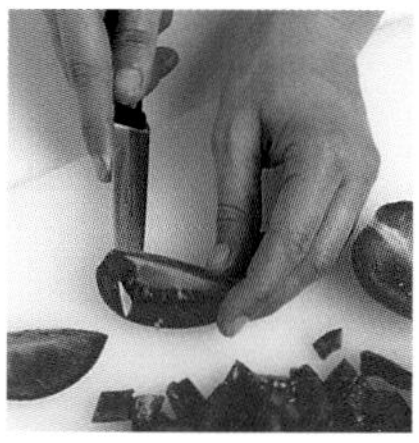

2 Put the tomatoes and oil in a bowl, adding salt and pepper to taste, and stir well. Cover and leave at room temperature for 1–2 hours to let the flavours mingle.

3 Cook the spaghetti or your chosen pasta according to the packet instructions, then drain well.

4 Taste the sauce to check the seasoning before tossing it with the hot pasta. Sprinkle with the cheese and serve immediately.

Rosemary Risotto with Borlotti Beans

Select a high-quality risotto in a subtle flavour as the base for this recipe. The savoury beans, heady rosemary and creamy mascarpone will transform a simple product into a feast. For an even more authentic risotto flavour, substitute half the water with dry white wine. Serve with a simple salad of rocket (arugula) and Parmesan shavings dressed with balsamic vinegar and plenty of freshly ground black pepper.

SERVES THREE TO FOUR

400g/14oz can borlotti beans

275g/10oz packet vegetable or chicken risotto

60ml/4 tbsp mascarpone cheese

5ml/1 tsp finely chopped fresh rosemary

1 Drain the beans, rinse under cold water and drain again. Process about two-thirds of the beans to a fairly coarse purée in a food processor or blender. Set the remaining beans aside.

2 Make up the risotto according to the packet instructions, using the suggested quantity of water.

3 Immediately the rice is cooked, stir in the bean purée. Add the reserved beans, with the mascarpone and rosemary, then season to taste. Stir thoroughly, then cover and leave to stand for about 5 minutes so that the risotto absorbs the flavours fully.

VARIATION

Fresh thyme or marjoram could be used for this risotto instead of rosemary, if you like. One of the great virtues of risotto is that it lends itself well to many variations. Experiment with plain or saffron risotto and add different herbs to make your own speciality dish.

Mussel Risotto

The addition of freshly cooked mussels, aromatic coriander and a little cream to a packet of instant risotto can turn a simple meal into a decadent treat. Serve with a side salad for a splendid supper. Other types of cooked shellfish, such as clams or prawns (shrimp), can be used instead of mussels.

SERVES THREE TO FOUR

900g/2lb fresh mussels

275g/10oz packet risotto

30ml/2 tbsp chopped fresh coriander (cilantro)

30ml/2 tbsp double (heavy) cream

1 Scrub the mussels, discarding any that do not close when sharply tapped. Place in a large pan. Add 120ml/4fl oz/½ cup water and seasoning, then bring to the boil. Cover the pan and cook the mussels, shaking the pan occasionally, for 4–5 minutes, until they have opened. Drain, reserving the liquid and discarding any that have not opened. Shell most of the mussels, reserving a few in their shells for garnish. Strain the mussel liquid.

2 Make up the packet risotto according to the instructions, using the cooking liquid from the mussels and making it up to the required volume with water.

3 When the risotto is about three-quarters cooked, add the mussels to the pan. Add the coriander and re-cover the pan without stirring in these ingredients.

4 Remove the risotto from the heat, stir in the cream, cover and leave to rest for a few minutes. Spoon into a warmed serving dish, garnish with the reserved mussels in their shells, and serve.

COOK'S TIP

For a super-quick mussel risotto, use cooked mussels in their shells – the type sold vacuum packed ready to reheat. Just reheat them according to the packet instructions and add to the made risotto with the coriander and cream.

Spiced Lentils

The combination of lentils, tomatoes and cheese is widely used in Mediterranean cooking. The tang of feta cheese complements the slightly earthy flavour of the attractive dark lentils. True Puy lentils come from the region of France, Le Puy, which has a unique climate and volcanic soil in which they thrive.

SERVES FOUR

250g/9oz/1½ cups Puy lentils

200g/7oz feta cheese

75ml/5 tbsp sun-dried tomato purée (paste)

small handful of fresh chervil or flat leaf parsley, chopped, plus extra to garnish

1 Place the lentils in a heavy pan with 600ml/1 pint/2½ cups water. Bring to the boil, reduce the heat and cover the pan. Simmer gently for about 20 minutes, until the lentils are just tender and most of the water has been absorbed.

2 Crumble half the feta cheese into the pan. Add the sun-dried tomato purée, chopped chervil or flat leaf parsley and a little salt and freshly ground black pepper. Heat through for 1 minute.

3 Transfer the lentil mixture and juices to warmed plates or bowls. Crumble the remaining feta cheese on top and sprinkle with the fresh herbs to garnish. Serve the lentils immediately.

Jansson's Temptation

This traditional Swedish gratin is utterly moreish. The name probably does not refer to a specific Jansson but means "everyone's temptation", as Jansson is a common Swedish surname.

SERVES FOUR TO SIX

1 Preheat the oven to 200°C/400°F/Gas 6. Cut the potatoes into thin slices, then cut the slices into matchstick strips. Toss with salt and black pepper and sprinkle half of them in the base of a greased shallow 1.5 litre/2½pint/6¼ cup baking dish.

2 Lay half of the onions on top of the potatoes, and season with black pepper. Lay the anchovies on top of the onions, then add the remaining onions and potatoes.

3 Mix the cream with 30ml/2 tbsp cold water and pour over the potatoes and onions. Cover with foil and bake for 1 hour, then reduce the oven temperature to 180°C/350°F/Gas 4 and uncover the dish. Bake for a further 40–50 minutes, or until the potatoes are golden and tender when tested with a knife.

900g/2lb potatoes

2 large, sweet onions, sliced

2 × 50g/2oz cans anchovies in olive oil, drained

450ml/¾ pint/scant 2 cups whipping cream or half and half double (heavy) and single (light) cream

Baked Salmon with Caraway Seeds

This classic Czech way of cooking salmon is very easy and gives excellent results. The fish cooks in its own juices, taking on the lovely warm flavour of the caraway seeds. Serve sprinkled with flat leaf parsley and wedges of lemon for squeezing over the fish.

SERVES FOUR

1.8kg/4lb whole salmon, cleaned

115g/4oz/½ cup butter, melted

2.5–5ml/½–1 tsp caraway seeds

45ml/3 tbsp lemon juice

1 Preheat the oven to 180°C/350°F/Gas 4. Scale the salmon, remove the head and tail and slice off the fins with a sharp knife, then cut the fish in half lengthways.

2 Place the salmon, skin-side down, in a lightly greased roasting pan. Brush with the melted butter. Season with salt and pepper, sprinkle over the caraway seeds and drizzle with lemon juice.

3 Cover the salmon loosely with foil and bake for 25 minutes. Remove it from the oven, lift off the foil and test the fish. (The flesh should be opaque and flake easily. Return to the oven if necessary.)

4 Remove the foil and carefully lift the fish on to a serving plate. It may be served hot or cold.

Tonno con Piselli

This Jewish Italian dish of fresh tuna and peas is especially enjoyed at Passover, which falls in spring. Before the days of the freezer, little peas were only eaten at this time of year when they were in season. At other times of the year chickpeas were used instead – they give a heartier result.

SERVES FOUR

350g/12oz tuna steaks

600ml/1 pint/2½ cups fresh tomato sauce

350g/12oz/3 cups fresh shelled or frozen peas

45ml/3 tbsp chopped fresh flat leaf parsley

1 Preheat the oven to 190°C/375°F/Gas 5. Sprinkle the tuna steaks on each side with salt and plenty of freshly ground black pepper and place in a shallow ovenproof dish, in a single layer.

2 Bring the tomato sauce to the boil, then add the fresh shelled or frozen peas and chopped fresh flat leaf parsley. Pour the sauce and peas evenly over the fish steaks in the ovenproof dish and bake in the preheated oven, uncovered, for about 20 minutes, or until the fish is tender. Serve the fish, sauce and peas immediately, straight from the dish.

VARIATION

This recipe works well with other types and cuts of fish. Use tuna fillets in place of the steaks or try different fish steaks, such as salmon or swordfish.

Sea Bass in a Salt Crust

Baking fish in a crust of sea salt seals in and enhances its flavour. Any firm fish can be cooked in this way. Decorate with a garnish of seaweed or blanched samphire and lemon slices, and break open the crust at the table to release the glorious aroma. Serve the fish with baby new potatoes roasted with olive oil and a sprinkling of dried rosemary, and steamed green vegetables such as broccoli or green beans.

SERVES FOUR

1 sea bass, about 1kg/2¼lb, cleaned and scaled

1 sprig each of fresh fennel, rosemary and thyme

mixed peppercorns

2kg/4½lb coarse sea salt

1 Preheat the oven to 240°C/475°F/Gas 9. Fill the cavity of the fish with the sprigs of fresh fennel, rosemary and thyme, and grind over some of the mixed peppercorns.

2 Spread half the salt in an ovenproof dish (ideally oval) and lay the sea bass on it. Cover the fish all over with a 1cm/½in layer of salt, pressing it down firmly. Moisten the salt lightly by spraying with water from an atomizer. Bake the fish for 30–40 minutes, until the salt crust is just beginning to colour.

3 Bring the sea bass to the table in its salt crust. Use a sharp knife to break open the crust and cut into four portions.

Fish with Tomato and Pine Nuts

Whole fish marinated in lemon juice and cooked with pine nuts in a spicy tomato sauce makes a perfect dish for a special meal. The fish may be cooked and served with head and tail on, as here, or if you like, with these removed. For a pretty finish, sprinkle the fish with chopped fresh flat leaf parsely just before serving – it contrasts beautifully with the rich red sauce.

SERVES SIX TO EIGHT

1–1.5kg/2¼–3¼lb fish, such as snapper, cleaned, with head and tail left on

juice of 2 lemons

65g/2½oz/scant ¾ cup pine nuts, toasted

350ml/12fl oz/1½ cups spicy tomato sauce

1 Prick the fish all over with a fork and rub with 2.5ml/½ tsp salt. Put the fish in a roasting pan or large dish and pour over the lemon juice. Leave to stand for 2 hours.

2 Preheat the oven to 180°C/350°F/Gas 4. Sprinkle half of the pine nuts over the base of an ovenproof dish, top with half of the sauce, then add the fish and its marinade. Add the remaining tomato sauce and the remaining pine nuts.

3 Cover the ovenproof dish tightly with a lid or foil and bake in the preheated oven for 30 minutes, or until the fish is tender. Serve the fish immediately, straight from the dish.

Drunken Chicken

In this traditional Chinese dish, cooked chicken is marinated in sherry, fresh root ginger and spring onions for several days. Because of the lengthy preparation time, it is important to use a very fresh bird from a reputable supplier. Fresh herbs can be added as an additional garnish, if you like.

SERVES FOUR TO SIX

1 chicken, about 1.3kg/3lb

1cm/½in piece of fresh root ginger, thinly sliced

2 spring onions (scallions), trimmed, plus extra to garnish

300ml/½ pint/1¼ cups dry sherry

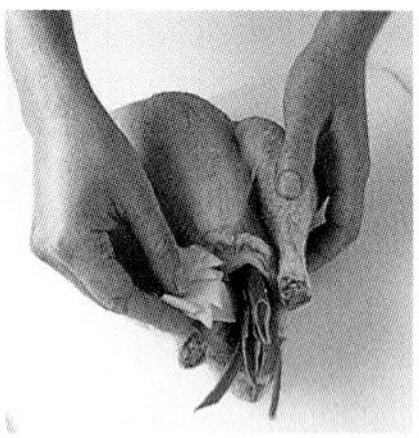

1 Rinse and dry the chicken inside and out. Place the ginger and spring onions in the body cavity. Put the chicken in a large pan or flameproof casserole and just cover with water. Bring to the boil, skim off any scum and cook for 15 minutes.

2 Turn off the heat, cover the pan or casserole tightly and leave the chicken in the cooking liquid for 3–4 hours, by which time it will be cooked. Drain well, reserving the stock. Pour 300ml/½ pint/1¼ cups of the stock into a jug (pitcher).

3 Remove the skin and cut the chicken into neat pieces. Divide each leg into a drumstick and thigh. Make two more portions from the wings and some of the breast. Finally, cut away the remainder of the breast pieces (still on the bone) and divide each piece into two even-size portions.

4 Arrange the chicken portions in a shallow dish. Rub salt into the chicken and cover with clear film (plastic wrap). Leave in a cool place for several hours or overnight in the refrigerator.

5 Later, lift off any fat from the stock, add the sherry and pour over the chicken. Cover again and leave in the refrigerator to marinate for 2–3 days, turning occasionally.

6 When ready to serve, cut the chicken through the bone into chunky pieces and arrange on a large serving platter. Garnish the chicken with spring onion shreds.

VARIATION

To serve as a cocktail snack, take the meat off the bones, cut it into bitesize pieces, then spear each piece on a cocktail stick (toothpick).

Turkey Patties

So much better than store-bought burgers, these light patties are delicious served hamburger-style in split and toasted buns with relish, salad leaves and chunky fries. They can also be made using minced chicken, lamb, pork or beef. If you are making them for children, shape the mixture into 12 equal-sized rounds and serve in mini-rolls or in rounds stamped out from sliced bread.

SERVES SIX

675g/1½lb minced (ground) turkey

1 small red onion, finely chopped

small handful of fresh thyme leaves

30ml/2 tbsp lime-flavoured olive oil

1 Mix together the turkey, onion, thyme, 15ml/1 tbsp of the oil and seasoning. Cover and chill for up to 4 hours to let the flavours infuse (steep), then divide the mixture into six equal portions and shape into round patties.

2 Preheat a griddle pan. Brush the patties with half of the remaining lime-flavoured olive oil, then place them on the pan and cook for 10–12 minutes. Turn the patties over, brush with more oil, and cook for 10–12 minutes on the second side, or until cooked right through. Serve the patties immediately.

VARIATION

As well as using other minced (ground) meat, you could try chopped oregano or parsley in place of the thyme, and lemon-flavoured oil instead of lime.

North African Lamb

This dish is full of contrasting flavours that create a rich, spicy and fruity main course. For best results, use lamb that still retains some fat, as this will help keep the meat moist and succulent during roasting. Serve the lamb with couscous or mixed white and wild rice, sprinkled with chopped coriander (cilantro). Roasted chunks of red and yellow (bell) peppers, aubergine (eggplant) and courgettes (zucchini), cooked in the oven with the lamb, complete the meal.

SERVES FOUR

675g/1½lb lamb fillet or shoulder steaks, cut into chunky pieces

5 small onions

7.5ml/1½ tsp harissa

115g/4oz ready-to-eat pitted prunes, halved

1 Preheat the oven to 200°C/400°F/Gas 6. Season the lamb with salt and pepper. Heat a frying pan, preferably non-stick, and cook the lamb on all sides until beginning to brown. Transfer to a roasting pan, reserving any fat in the frying pan.

2 Peel the onions and cut each into six wedges. Toss with the lamb and roast for about 30-40 minutes, until the lamb is cooked through and the onions are deep golden brown.

3 Tip the lamb and onions back into the frying pan. Mix the harissa with 250ml/8fl oz/1 cup boiling water and add to the roasting pan. Scrape up any residue in the pan and pour the mixture over the lamb and onions. Stir in the prunes and heat until just simmering. Cover and simmer for 5 minutes, then serve.

Lamb Steaks with Redcurrant Glaze

This classic, simple dish is absolutely delicious and is an excellent, quick recipe for cooking on the barbecue. The tangy flavour of redcurrants is a traditional accompaniment to lamb. It is good served with new potatoes and fresh garden peas tossed in butter.

SERVES FOUR

4 large fresh rosemary sprigs

4 lamb leg steaks

75ml/5 tbsp redcurrant jelly

30ml/2 tbsp raspberry or red wine vinegar

1 Reserve the tips of the rosemary and finely chop the remaining leaves. Rub the chopped rosemary, salt and pepper all over the lamb.

2 Preheat the grill (broiler). Heat the redcurrant jelly gently in a small pan with 30ml/2 tbsp water and a little seasoning. Stir in the vinegar.

3 Place the lamb steaks on a foil-lined grill (broiler) rack and brush with a little of the redcurrant glaze. Cook under the grill for about 5 minutes on each side, until deep golden, brushing frequently with more redcurrant glaze.

4 Transfer the lamb to warmed plates. Tip any juices from the foil into the remaining glaze and heat through gently. Pour the glaze over the lamb and serve, garnished with the reserved rosemary sprigs.

Beef Patties with Onions and Peppers

This is a firm family favourite. It is easy to make and delicious, and it can be varied by adding other vegetables, such as sliced red peppers, broccoli or mushrooms. These patties are very versatile and can be served in a variety of ways – with chunky home-made chips (fries), with crusty bread, or with rice and a ready-made tomato sauce.

SERVES FOUR

500g/1¼lb lean minced (ground) beef

4 onions, 1 finely chopped and 3 sliced

30ml/2 tbsp garlic-flavoured olive oil or olive oil

2–3 green (bell) peppers, seeded and sliced lengthways into strips

1 Place the minced beef, chopped onion and 15ml/1 tbsp garlic-flavoured oil in a bowl and mix well. Season well and form into four large or eight small patties.

2 Heat the remaining oil in a large non-stick pan, then add the patties and cook on both sides until browned. Sprinkle over 15ml/1 tbsp water and add a little seasoning.

3 Cover the patties with the sliced onions and peppers. Sprinkle in another 15ml/1 tbsp water and a little seasoning, then cover the pan. Reduce the heat to very low and braise for 20–30 minutes.

4 When the onions are turning golden brown, remove the pan from the heat. Serve the patties with onions and peppers.

Steak with Warm Tomato Salsa

A refreshing, tangy salsa of tomatoes, spring onions and balsamic vinegar makes a colourful topping for chunky, pan-fried steaks. Choose rump, sirloin or fillet – whichever is your favourite – and if you do not have a non-stick pan, grill the steak instead for the same length of time. Serve with potato wedges and a mixed leaf salad with a mustard dressing.

SERVES TWO

2 steaks, about 2cm/ ¾in thick

4 large plum tomatoes

2 spring onions (scallions)

30ml/2 tbsp balsamic vinegar

1 Trim any excess fat from the steaks, then season on both sides with salt and pepper. Heat a non-stick frying pan and cook the steaks for about 3 minutes on each side for medium rare. Cook for a little longer if you like your steak well cooked.

2 Meanwhile, put the tomatoes in a heatproof bowl, cover with boiling water and leave for 1–2 minutes, until the skins start to split. Drain and peel the tomatoes, then halve them and scoop out the seeds. Dice the tomato flesh. Thinly slice the spring onions.

3 Transfer the steaks to plates and keep warm. Add the vegetables, balsamic vinegar, 30ml/2 tbsp water and a little seasoning to the cooking juices in the pan and stir briefly until warm, scraping up any meat residue. Spoon the salsa over the steaks to serve.

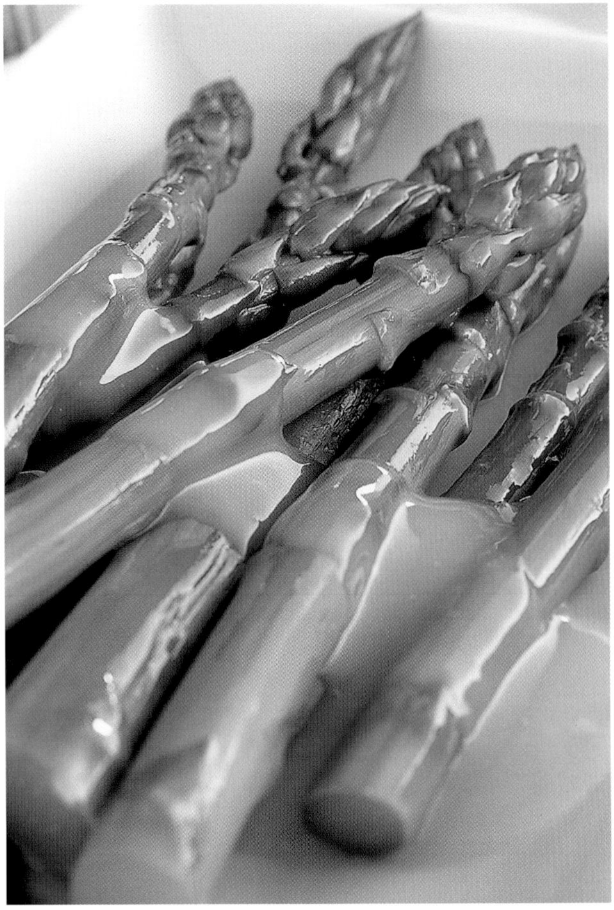

Salads and Side Dishes

A FEW CAREFULLY CHOSEN INGREDIENTS CAN BE BROUGHT TOGETHER TO CREATE MOUTHWATERING SIDE DISHES AND ACCOMPANIMENTS THAT WILL COMPLEMENT AND ENHANCE ANY MAIN DISH. THIS COLLECTION OF TASTY AND COLOURFUL COMBINATIONS OF VEGETABLES MAKES HEALTHY EATING A TEMPTING TREAT.

Anchovy and Roasted Pepper Salad

Sweet peppers, salty anchovies and plenty of garlic make an intensely flavoured salad that is delicious with meat, poultry or cheese. It also makes a tasty snack with olive bread. If you find that canned anchovies are too salty for your liking, you can reduce their saltiness by soaking them in milk for 20 minutes. Drain off the oil first and after soaking drain and rinse them in cold water.

SERVES FOUR

2 red, 2 orange and 2 yellow (bell) peppers, halved and seeded

50g/2oz can anchovies in olive oil

2 garlic cloves

45ml/3 tbsp balsamic vinegar

1 Preheat the oven to 200°C/400°F/Gas 6. Place the peppers, cut-side down, in a roasting pan. Roast for 30-40 minutes, until the skins are charred. Transfer the peppers to a bowl, cover with clear film (plastic wrap) and leave for 15 minutes.

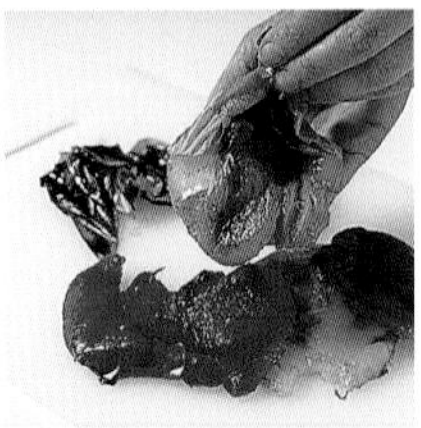

2 Peel the peppers, then cut them into chunky strips. Drain the anchovies and halve the fillets lengthways.

3 Slice the garlic as thinly as possible and place it in a large bowl. Stir in the olive oil, vinegar and a little pepper. Add the peppers and anchovies and use a spoon and fork to fold the ingredients together. Cover and chill until ready to serve.

Potato and Olive Salad

This delicious salad is simple and zesty – the perfect choice for lunch, as an accompaniment, or as an appetizer. Similar in appearance to flat leaf parsley, fresh coriander has a distinctive pungent, almost spicy flavour. It is widely used in India, the Middle and Far East and in eastern Mediterranean countries. This potato salad is particularly good served as part of a brunch.

SERVES FOUR

8 large new potatoes

45–60ml/3–4 tbsp garlic-flavoured oil and vinegar dressing

60–90ml/4–6 tbsp chopped fresh herbs, such as coriander (cilantro) and chives

10–15 dry-fleshed black Mediterranean olives

1 Cut the new potatoes into chunks. Put them in a pan, pour in water to cover and add a pinch of salt. Bring to the boil, then reduce the heat and cook gently for about 10 minutes, or until the potatoes are just tender. Drain well and leave in a colander to dry thoroughly and cool slightly.

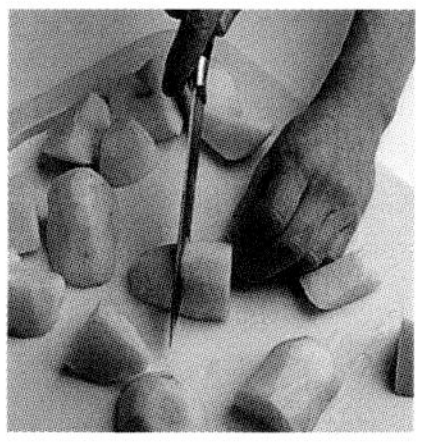

2 When they are cool enough to handle, chop the potatoes and put them in a serving bowl.

3 Drizzle the garlic dressing over the potatoes. Toss well and sprinkle with the chopped fresh coriander and chives, and black olives. Chill in the refrigerator for at least 1 hour before serving.

EXTRAS

Add a pinch of ground cumin or a sprinkling of roasted whole cumin seeds to spice up the salad.

Globe Artichokes with Green Beans and Garlic Dressing

Piquant garlic dressing or creamy aioli go perfectly with these lightly-cooked vegetables. Serve lemon wedges with the artichokes so that their juice may be squeezed over to taste. The vegetables can also be garnished with finely shredded lemon rind. Artichokes should feel heavy for their size – make sure that the inner leaves are wrapped tightly round the choke and the heart inside.

SERVES FOUR TO SIX

225g/8oz green beans

3 small globe artichokes

15ml/1 tbsp lemon-flavoured olive oil

250ml/8fl oz/1 cup garlic dressing or aioli

1 Cook the beans in boiling water for 1–2 minutes, until slightly softened. Drain well.

2 Trim the artichoke stalks close to the base. Cook them in a large pan of salted water for about 30 minutes, or until you can easily pull away a leaf from the base. Drain well.

3 Using a sharp knife, halve them lengthways and ease out their chokes using a teaspoon.

4 Arrange the artichokes and beans on serving plates and drizzle with the oil. Season with coarse salt and a little pepper. Spoon the garlic dressing or aioli into the hearts and serve warm.

5 To eat the artichokes, pull the leaves from the base one at a time and use to scoop a little of the dressing. It is only the fleshy end of each leaf that is eaten as well as the base, bottom or "fond".

Asparagus with Lemon Sauce

Sometimes less is more: here a simple egg and lemon dressing brings out the best in asparagus. Serve the asparagus as an appetizer or side dish; alternatively, enjoy it for a light supper, with bread and butter to mop up the juices. When buying asparagus, look for bright coloured firm spears with tight buds – avoid those with tough woody stems. Choose roughly even-sized spears for uniform cooking.

SERVES FOUR

675g/1½lb asparagus, tough ends removed, and tied in a bundle

15ml/1 tbsp cornflour (cornstarch)

2 egg yolks

juice of 1½ lemons

1 Cook the bundle of asparagus in a tall pan of lightly salted, boiling water for 7–10 minutes.

2 Drain well and arrange the asparagus in a serving dish. Reserve 200ml/7fl oz/scant 1 cup of the cooking liquid.

3 Blend the cornflour with the cooled, reserved cooking liquid and place in a small pan. Bring to the boil, stirring constantly, and cook over a gentle heat until the sauce thickens slightly. Remove the pan from the heat and leave to cool slightly.

4 Beat the egg yolks thoroughly with the lemon juice and gradually stir into the cooled sauce. Cook over a very low heat, stirring constantly, until the sauce is fairly thick. Be careful not to overheat the sauce or it may curdle. As soon as the sauce has thickened, remove the pan from the heat and continue stirring for 1 minute. Taste and season with salt. Leave the sauce to cool slightly.

5 Stir the cooled lemon sauce, then pour a little over the cooked asparagus. Cover and chill in the refrigerator for at least 2 hours before serving with the rest of the sauce to accompany.

COOK'S TIP

For a slightly less tangy sauce, add a little caster (superfine) sugar with the salt in step 4.

Minty Broad Beans with Lemon

Young, tender broad beans have a sweet, mild taste and are delicious served in a simple salad. Take advantage of them when they're in season and make them into this fresh, zesty dish. Green peas – either fresh or frozen – are also delicious served in the same way, but you don't need to peel off their already tender skins.

SERVES FOUR

450g/1lb broad (fava) beans, thawed if frozen

grated rind and juice of 1 unwaxed lemon

1 small bunch of fresh mint, roughly chopped

FROM THE STORECUPBOARD

30ml/2 tbsp garlic-infused olive oil

salt and ground black pepper

1 Using your fingers, slip the grey skins off the broad beans and discard – this takes a little time but the result is well worthwhile. Cook the beans in salted boiling water for 3–4 minutes, or until just tender.

2 Drain well and toss with the oil, lemon rind and juice, and mint. Season with salt and pepper, and serve immediately.

COOK'S TIP

When using fresh broad beans, it is easier to cook them first, then run them under cold water before slipping off their skins. Quickly blanch the skinned beans in boiling water to re-heat them.

Gingered Carrot Salad

This fresh and zesty salad is ideal served as an accompaniment to simple grilled chicken or fish. Some food processors have an attachment that can be used to cut the carrots into batons, which makes quick work of the preparation, but even cutting them by hand doesn't take too long. Fresh root ginger goes perfectly with sweet carrots, and the tiny black poppy seeds not only add taste and texture, but also look stunning against the bright orange of the carrots.

SERVES FOUR

350g/12oz carrots, peeled and cut into fine matchsticks

2.5cm/1in piece of fresh root ginger, peeled and grated

15ml/1 tbsp poppy seeds

FROM THE STORECUPBOARD

30ml/2 tbsp garlic-infused olive oil

salt and ground black pepper

1 Put the carrots in a bowl and stir in the oil and grated ginger. Cover and chill for at least 30 minutes, to allow the flavours to develop.

2 Season the salad with salt and pepper to taste. Stir in the poppy seeds just before serving.

VARIATION

To make a parsnip and sesame seed salad, replace the carrots with parsnips and blanch in boiling salted water for 1 minute before combining with the oil and ginger. Replace the poppy seeds with the same quantity of sesame seeds.

Baked Winter Squash with Tomatoes

Acorn, butternut or Hubbard squash can all be used in this simple recipe. Serve the squash as a light main course, with warm crusty bread, or as a side dish for grilled meat or poultry. Canned chopped tomatoes with herbs are used in this recipe. A variety of flavoured canned tomatoes are now available including garlic, onion and olive – they are ideal for adding a combination of flavours when time is short.

SERVES FOUR TO SIX

1 Preheat the oven to 160°C/325°F/Gas 3. Heat the oil in a pan and cook the pumpkin or squash slices, in batches, until golden brown, removing them from the pan as they are cooked.

2 Add the tomatoes and cook over a medium-high heat until the mixture is of a sauce consistency. Stir in the rosemary and season to taste with salt and pepper.

3 Layer the pumpkin slices and tomatoes in an ovenproof dish, ending with a layer of tomatoes. Bake for 35 minutes, or until the top is lightly glazed and beginning to turn golden brown, and the pumpkin is tender. Serve immediately.

45ml/3 tbsp garlic-flavoured olive oil

1kg/2¼lb pumpkin or orange winter squash, peeled and sliced

2 x 400g/14oz cans chopped tomatoes with herbs

2–3 fresh rosemary sprigs, stems removed and leaves chopped

Stewed Okra with Tomatoes and Coriander

This is a favourite Middle-Eastern way to prepare okra. Add wedges of lemon as a garnish so that their juice can be squeezed over the vegetables to taste. Okra, also known as lady's fingers, are narrow green lantern-shaped pods. They contain a row of seeds that ooze a viscous liquid when cooked. This liquid acts as a natural thickener in a variety of curries and soups.

SERVES FOUR TO SIX

1 Heat the tomatoes and the cinnamon, cumin and cloves with half the coriander in a pan, then season to taste with salt and freshly ground black pepper and bring to the boil.

2 Add the okra and cook, stirring constantly, for 1–2 minutes. Reduce the heat to low, then simmer, stirring occasionally, for 20–30 minutes, until the okra is tender.

3 Taste for spicing and seasoning, and adjust if necessary, adding more of any one spice, salt or pepper to taste. Stir in the remaining coriander. Serve hot, warm or cold.

400g/14oz can chopped tomatoes with onions and garlic

generous pinch each of ground cinnamon, cumin and cloves

90ml/6 tbsp chopped fresh coriander (cilantro) leaves

800g/1¾lb okra

Tomato and Aubergine Gratin

This colourful, Mediterranean dish makes the perfect partner to grilled, pan-fried or baked meat or poultry. If you prefer, thinly sliced courgettes (zucchini) can be used in this dish instead of the aubergines (eggplants). Grill the courgettes for 10–15 minutes. Choose plum tomatoes if you can – they have fewer seeds than most round tomatoes, so are less watery and are ideal for cooking.

SERVES FOUR TO SIX

2 medium aubergines (eggplant), about 500g/1¼lb

90ml/6 tbsp olive oil

400g/14oz ripe tomatoes, sliced

40g/1½oz/½ cup freshly grated Parmesan cheese

1 Preheat the grill (broiler). Thinly slice the aubergines and arrange them in a single layer on a foil-lined grill rack. Brush the aubergine slices with some of the olive oil and grill (broil) for 15–20 minutes, turning once, until golden on both sides. Brush the second side with more olive oil after turning the slices.

2 Preheat the oven to 200°C/400°F/Gas 6. Toss the aubergine and tomato slices together in a bowl with a little seasoning, then pile them into a shallow, ovenproof dish. Drizzle with any remaining olive oil and sprinkle with the grated Parmesan cheese. Bake for 20 minutes, until the cheese is golden and the vegetables are hot. Serve the gratin immediately.

Baked Leek and Potato Gratin

Potatoes baked in a creamy cheese sauce make the ultimate comfort dish, and are particularly good served as an accompaniment to pork or fish dishes. When preparing leeks, separate the leaves and rinse them thoroughly under cold running water, because soil and grit often get caught between the layers and will spoil the finished dish.

SERVES FOUR TO SIX

900g/2lb medium potatoes, thinly sliced

2 large leeks, trimmed

200g/7oz ripe Brie or Camembert cheese, sliced

450ml/¾ pint/ scant 2 cups single (light) cream

1 Preheat the oven to 180°C/350°F/Gas 4. Cook the potatoes in plenty of lightly salted, boiling water for 3 minutes, until slightly softened, then drain. Cut the leeks into 1cm/½in lengths and blanch them in boiling water for 1 minute, until softened, then drain.

2 Turn half the potatoes into a shallow, ovenproof dish and spread them out to the edge. Cover with two-thirds of the leeks, then add the remaining potatoes. Tuck the slices of cheese and the remaining leeks in among the top layer of potatoes. Season with salt and pepper and pour the cream over.

3 Bake for 1 hour, until tender and golden. Cover with foil if the top starts to overbrown before the potatoes are tender.

Fennel, Potato and Garlic Mash

This flavoursome mash of potato, fennel and garlic goes well with practically all main dishes, whether fish, poultry or meat. Floury varieties of potato such as Pentland Squire, King Edward or Marfona are best for mashing as they produce a light fluffy result. Waxy potatoes are more suitable for baking, or for salads, as they produce a dense, rather starchy mash.

SERVES FOUR

800g/1¾lb potatoes, cut into chunks

2 large fennel bulbs

90ml/6 tbsp garlic-flavoured olive oil

120–150ml/4–5fl oz/ ½–⅔ cup milk or single (light) cream

1 Boil the potatoes in salted water for 20 minutes, until tender.

2 Meanwhile, trim and coarsely chop the fennel, reserving any feathery tops. Chop the tops and set them aside. Heat 30ml/2 tbsp of the oil in a heavy pan. Add the fennel, cover and cook over a low heat for 20–30 minutes, until soft but not browned.

3 Drain and mash the potatoes. Purée the fennel in a food mill or blender and beat it into the potato with the remaining oil.

4 Warm the milk or cream and beat sufficient into the potato and fennel to make a creamy, light mixture. Season to taste and reheat gently, then beat in any chopped fennel tops. Serve immediately.

Bubble and Squeak

Whether you have leftovers or cook this old-fashioned classic from fresh, be sure to give it a really good "squeak" in the pan so it turns a rich honey brown. Serve as an accompaniment to grilled pork chops or fried eggs, or simply serve with warm bread for a quick supper. If you prefer, cook the bubble and squeak in individual-sized portions – divide into four and form into patties before cooking.

SERVES FOUR

60ml/4 tbsp bacon fat or vegetable oil

1 medium onion, finely chopped

450g/1lb floury potatoes, cooked and mashed

225g/8oz cooked cabbage or Brussels sprouts, finely chopped

1 Heat 30ml/2 tbsp of the bacon fat or oil in a heavy frying pan. Add the onion and cook over a medium heat, stirring frequently, until softened but not browned.

2 In a large bowl, mix together the potatoes and cooked cabbage or sprouts and season with salt and plenty of pepper to taste.

3 Add the vegetables to the pan with the cooked onions, stir well, then press the vegetable mixture into a large, even cake.

4 Cook over a medium heat for about 15 minutes, until the cake is browned underneath.

5 Invert a large plate over the pan, and, holding it tightly against the pan, turn them both over together. Lift off the frying pan, return it to the heat and add the remaining bacon fat or oil. When hot, slide the cake back into the pan, browned side uppermost.

6 Cook over a medium heat for 10 minutes, or until the underside is golden brown. Serve hot, in wedges.

EXTRAS

When made with vegetables from a roast dinner, the mixture can be moistened with leftover gravy, making it bubble as it cooks and giving a really delicious savoury flavour.

Tandoori Rotis

Indian flat breads make a great accompaniment to richly flavoured stews. Traditionally, these breads would be baked in a tandoor, a clay oven that is heated with charcoal or wood. The oven becomes extremely hot, cooking the bread in minutes. Here, however, they are baked in a regular oven; they are ready when light brown bubbles appear on the surface.

MAKES SIX ROTIS

350g/12oz/3 cups atta or fine wholemeal (whole-wheat) flour

5ml/1 tsp salt

30–45ml/2–3 tbsp melted ghee or butter, for brushing

1 Sift the flour and salt into a large bowl. Add 250ml/8fl oz/1 cup water and mix to a soft dough. Knead on a lightly floured surface for 3–4 minutes, until smooth. Place the dough in a lightly oiled mixing bowl, cover with lightly oiled clear film (plastic wrap) and leave to rest for 1 hour.

2 Turn out on to a lightly floured surface. Divide the dough into six pieces and shape each piece into a ball. Press out into a larger round with the palm of your hand, cover with lightly oiled clear film (plastic wrap) and leave to rest for 10 minutes.

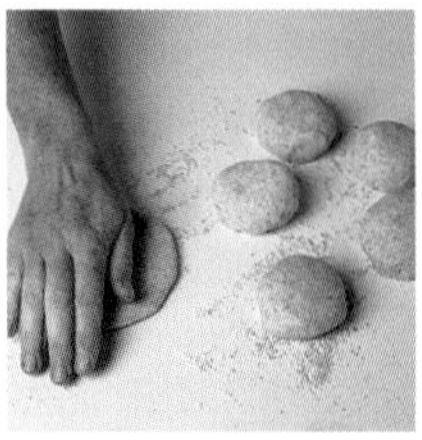

3 Meanwhile, preheat the oven to 230°C/450°F/Gas 8. Place three baking sheets in the oven to heat. Roll the rotis into 15cm/6in rounds, place two on each baking sheet and bake for 8–10 minutes. Brush with ghee or butter and serve warm.

Yemeni Sponge Flat Breads

These flat breads, known as *lahuhs* and made from a batter, are bubbly and soft. They are eaten with soups but are also good with salads, dips or cheese.

SERVES FOUR

15ml/1 tbsp dried active yeast

350g/12oz/ 3 cups plain (all-purpose) flour

5ml/1 tsp salt

50g/2oz/¼ cup butter, melted, or 60ml/4 tbsp vegetable oil

1 Measure 500ml/17fl oz/generous 2 cups lukewarm water. In a bowl, dissolve the dried yeast in about 75ml/5 tbsp of the water. Leave in a warm place for about 10 minutes, or until frothy.

2 Stir the remaining water, the flour, salt and melted butter or vegetable oil into the yeast mixture and mix until it forms a smooth batter. Cover with a clean dishtowel, then leave in a warm place for about 1 hour, until doubled in size.

3 Stir the thick, frothy batter and, if it seems too thick to ladle out, add a little extra water. Cover and leave the batter to stand in a warm place for about 1 hour.

4 Cook the flat breads in a non-stick frying pan. Ladle 45–60ml/ 3–4 tbsp of batter (or less for smaller breads) into the pan and cook over a low heat until the top is bubbling and the colour has changed. (Traditionally these breads are cooked on only one side, but they can be turned over and the second side cooked for just a moment, if you like.)

5 Remove the cooked flat bread from the frying pan with a spatula and keep warm in a clean dishtowel. Continue cooking until you have used up all the remaining batter.

COOK'S TIP

Use two or three frying pans at the same time so that the flat breads are ready together and so can be eaten piping hot.

Tea-time Treats

HOME-BAKED CAKES AND SWEET SNACKS ARE THE ULTIMATE INDULGENCE BUT ARE VIEWED BY MANY AS TAKING TOO MUCH TIME AND EFFORT. HOWEVER, WITH JUST A FEW BASIC INGREDIENTS, YOU CAN WHIP UP FABULOUS SWEET TREATS. TRY DELICIOUSLY INDULGENT SNACKS SUCH AS ALL BUTTER COOKIES, CHEWY FLAPJACKS OR QUICK AND EASY TEABREAD.

Creamed Coconut Macaroons

Finely grated creamed coconut gives these soft-centred cookies a rich creaminess. Cooking the gooey mixture on baking parchment makes sure that the cookies are easily removed from the baking sheet. For a tangy flavour, add the grated rind of one lime to the mixture in step 2. The cooked macaroons can be stored in an airtight container for up to one week.

MAKES SIXTEEN TO EIGHTEEN

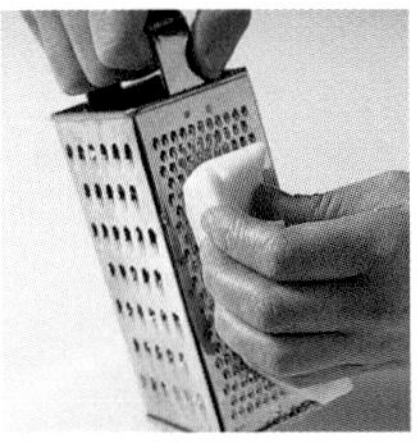

1 Preheat the oven to 180°C/350°F/Gas 4. Line a large baking sheet with baking parchment. Finely grate the creamed coconut.

2 Use an electric beater to whisk the egg whites in a large bowl until stiff. Whisk in the sugar, a little at a time, to make a stiff and glossy meringue. Fold in the grated creamed and desiccated coconut, using a large, metal spoon.

3 Place dessertspoonfuls of the mixture, spaced slightly apart, on the baking sheet. Bake for 15–20 minutes, until slightly risen and golden brown. Leave to cool on the parchment, then transfer to an airtight container.

50g/2oz creamed coconut, chilled

2 large (US extra large) egg whites

90g/3½oz/ ½ cup caster (superfine) sugar

75g/3oz/1 cup desiccated (dry unsweetened shredded) coconut

Almond Cookies

These short, light cookies have a melt-in-the-mouth texture. Their simplicity means they are endlessly versatile – irresistible with tea or coffee and stylish with special desserts.

MAKES ABOUT TWENTY-FOUR

115g/4oz/1 cup plain (all-purpose) flour

175g/6oz/1½ cups icing (confectioners') sugar, plus extra for dusting

50g/2oz/½ cup chopped almonds, plus halved almonds to decorate

115g/4oz/½ cup unsalted (sweet) butter, softened

1 Preheat the oven to 180°C/350°F/Gas 4. Combine the flour, sugar and chopped almonds in a bowl.

2 Put the softened unsalted butter in the centre of the flour and nut mixture and use a blunt knife or your fingertips to draw the dry ingredients into the butter until a dough is formed. Shape the dough into a ball.

3 Place the dough on a lightly floured surface and roll it out to a thickness of about 3mm/⅛in. Using a 7.5cm/3in cookie cutter, cut out about 24 rounds, re-rolling the dough as necessary. Place the cookie rounds on baking sheets, leaving a little space between them. Bake the cookies for about 25 minutes, until pale golden.

4 Leave the cookies on the baking sheet for 10 minutes, then transfer to wire racks to cool. Dust thickly with sifted icing sugar before serving, decorated with halved almonds.

COOK'S TIP

Use different-shaped cutters to make these cookies look even more interesting. Hearts, stars and crescents are three shapes that you might like to try.

Golden Ginger Macaroons

Macaroons are classic no-fuss cookies – easy to whisk up in minutes from the minimum ingredients and always acceptable. A hint of ginger makes this recipe that bit different. For a darker colour and slightly richer flavour, use soft dark brown sugar instead. Bake these biscuits on non-stick baking trays or on a baking tray lined with baking parchment to prevent them from sticking.

MAKES EIGHTEEN TO TWENTY

1 Preheat the oven to 180°C/350°F/Gas 4. In a large, grease-free bowl, whisk the egg white until stiff and standing in peaks, but not dry and crumbly, then whisk in the brown sugar.

2 Sprinkle the ground almonds and ginger over the whisked egg white and gently fold them together.

3 Using two teaspoons, place spoonfuls of the mixture on baking trays, leaving plenty of space between each. Bake for about 20 minutes, until pale golden brown and just turning crisp.

4 Leave to cool slightly on the baking trays before transferring to a wire rack to cool completely.

1 egg white

75g/3oz/scant ½ cup soft light brown sugar

115g/4oz/1 cup ground almonds

5ml/1 tsp ground ginger

VARIATION

Other ground nuts, such as hazelnuts or walnuts, are good alternatives to the almonds. Ground cinnamon or mixed (apple pie) spice can be used instead of the ginger, if liked.

Nutty Nougat

Nougat is an almost magical sweetmeat (candy) that emerges from honey-flavoured meringue made with boiled syrup. The sweet, nutty, chewy texture makes it a perfect sweet treat with a cup of tea, and makes an interesting alternative to the more usual cookie or slice of cake.

MAKES ABOUT 500G/1¼ LB

1 Line a 17.5cm/7in square cake tin (pan) with rice paper. Place the sugar, honey or syrup and 60ml/4 tbsp water in a large, heavy pan and heat gently, stirring frequently, until the sugar has completely dissolved.

2 Bring the syrup to the boil and boil gently to the soft crack stage (when the syrup dropped into cold water separates into hard but not brittle threads) or 151°C/304°F on a sugar thermometer.

3 Meanwhile, whisk the egg white until very stiff, but not crumbly, then slowly drizzle in the syrup while whisking constantly.

4 Quickly stir in the nuts and pour the mixture into the prepared tin. Leave to cool but, before the nougat becomes too hard, cut it into squares. Store in an airtight container.

225g/8oz/generous 1 cup granulated sugar

225g/8oz/1 cup clear honey or golden (light corn) syrup

1 large (US extra large) egg white

115g/4oz/1 cup flaked (sliced) almonds or chopped pistachio nuts, roasted

All Butter Cookies

Crisp, buttery cookies make a perfect mid-afternoon snack served with a cup of coffee or tea. These cookies are known as "refrigerator cookies" because the mixture is chilled until it is firm enough to cut neatly into thin slices. The dough can be frozen and, when thawed enough to slice, can be freshly baked, but do allow a little extra cooking time.

MAKES TWENTY-EIGHT TO THIRTY

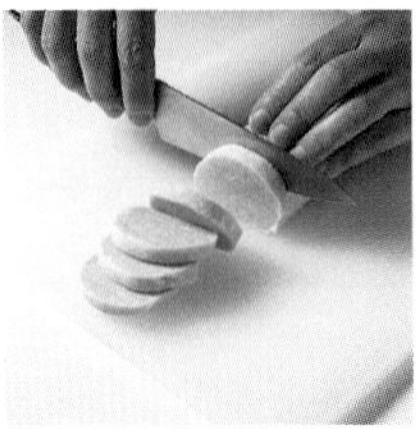

1 Put the flour in a food processor. Add the butter and process until the mixture resembles coarse breadcrumbs. Add the icing sugar and vanilla, and process until the mixture comes together to form a dough. Knead lightly and shape into a thick sausage, 30cm/12in long and 5cm/2in in diameter. Wrap and chill for at least 1 hour, until firm.

2 Preheat the oven to 200°C/400°F/Gas 6. Grease two baking sheets. Using a sharp knife, cut 5mm/¼in thick slices from the dough and space them slightly apart on the baking sheet.

3 Bake for 8–10 minutes, alternating the position of the baking sheets in the oven halfway through cooking, if necessary, until the biscuits are cooked evenly and have just turned pale golden around the edges. Leave for 5 minutes, then transfer to a wire rack to cool. Serve dusted with icing sugar.

275g/10oz/2½ cups plain (all-purpose) flour

200g/7oz/scant 1 cup unsalted (sweet) butter

90g/3½oz/scant 1 cup icing (confectioners') sugar, plus extra for dusting

10ml/2 tsp vanilla essence (extract)

Almond Cigars

These simple, Moroccan-inspired pastries can be prepared in minutes. They are perfect served with strong black coffee or black tea, or as an after-dinner treat. They are also delicious served with traditional sweet Moroccan mint tea. To serve, the pastries look very pretty sprinkled with a little icing (confectioners') sugar as a simple finishing touch.

MAKES EIGHT TO TWELVE

250g/9oz marzipan

1 egg, lightly beaten

8–12 sheets filo pastry

melted butter, for brushing

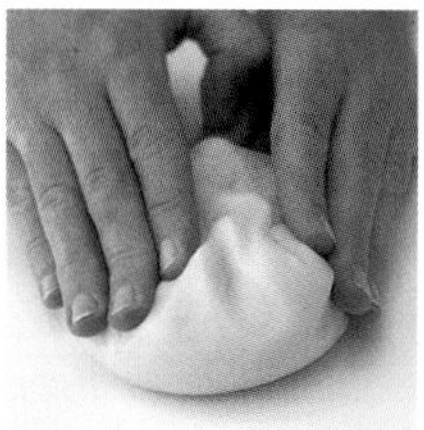

1 Knead the marzipan until soft and pliable, then put it in a mixing bowl and mix in the lightly beaten egg. Chill in the refrigerator for 1–2 hours.

2 Preheat the oven to 190°C/375°F/Gas 5. Lightly grease a baking sheet. Place a sheet of filo pastry on a piece of greaseproof (waxed) paper, keeping the remaining pastry covered with a damp cloth, and brush with the melted butter.

3 Shape 30–45ml/2–3 tbsp of the almond paste into a cylinder and place at one end of the pastry. Fold the pastry over to enclose the ends of the paste, then roll up to form a cigar shape. Place on the baking sheet and make 7–11 more cigars in the same way.

4 Bake the pastries in the preheated oven for about 15 minutes, or until golden brown in colour. Transfer to a wire rack to cool before serving.

Rich Chocolate Biscuit Slice

This dark chocolate refrigerator cake is packed with crisp biscuit pieces and chunks of white chocolate for colour and flavour contrast. The slice is perfect served with strong coffee, either as a tea-time treat or in place of dessert. Once set, cut the cake into slices and store them in an airtight container in the refrigerator until ready to serve.

SERVES EIGHT TO TEN

275g/10oz fruit and nut plain (semisweet) chocolate

130g/4½oz/ 9 tbsp unsalted (sweet) butter

90g/3½oz digestive biscuits (graham crackers)

90g/3½oz white chocolate

1 Grease and line the base and sides of a 450g/1lb loaf tin (pan) with baking parchment. Break the fruit and nut chocolate into pieces and place in a heatproof bowl with the butter. Place the bowl over a pan of barely simmering water and stir the chocolate gently until it is melted and smooth. Remove the bowl from the pan and leave to cool for 20 minutes.

2 Break the biscuits into small pieces. Finely chop the white chocolate. Stir the biscuits and white chocolate into the melted mixture until evenly combined. Turn the mixture into the prepared tin and pack down gently. Chill for about 2 hours, or until set. Cut the mixture into slices.

Orange and Pecan Scones

Serve these nutty orange scones with traditional English orange or lemon curd or, for a simple snack, fresh and warm with unsalted (sweet) butter. Scones are best served on the day they are made, or they can be frozen.

MAKES TEN

1 Preheat the oven to 220°C/425°F/Gas 7. Grease a baking sheet. Put the flour in a food processor with a pinch of salt and add the butter. Process the mixture until it resembles coarse breadcrumbs.

2 Add the orange rind. Reserve 30ml/2 tbsp of the orange juice and make the remainder up to 120ml/4fl oz/½ cup with water. Add the nuts and the juice mixture to the processor, process very briefly to a firm dough, adding a little water if the dough feels dry.

3 Turn the dough out on to a lightly floured surface and roll out to 2cm/¾in thick. Cut out scones using a round cutter and transfer them to the baking sheet. Re-roll the trimmings and cut more scones. Brush the scones with the reserved juice and bake for 15–20 minutes, until golden. Transfer to a wire rack to cool.

225g/8oz/ 2 cups self-raising (self-rising) flour

50g/2oz/¼ cup unsalted (sweet) butter, chilled and diced

grated rind and juice of 1 orange

115g/4oz/1 cup pecan nuts, coarsely chopped

Chewy Flapjacks

Flapjacks are popular with adults and children alike and they are so quick and easy to make. For alternative versions of the basic recipe, stir in 50g/2oz/¼ cup finely chopped ready-to-eat dried apricots or sultanas (golden raisins). To make a really decadent treat, you can dip the cooled flapjack fingers into melted chocolate, to half cover.

MAKES TWELVE

175g/6oz/¾ cup unsalted (sweet) butter

50g/2oz/¼ cup caster (superfine) sugar

150g/5oz/generous ⅓ cup golden (light corn) syrup

250g/9oz/2¾ cups rolled oats

1 Preheat the oven to 180°C/350°F/Gas 4. Line the base and sides of a 20cm/8in square cake tin (pan) with baking parchment.

2 Mix the butter, sugar and syrup in a pan and heat gently until the butter has melted. Add the oats and stir until all the ingredients are combined. Turn the mixture into the tin and level the surface.

3 Bake the flapjacks for 15–20 minutes, until just beginning to turn golden. Leave to cool slightly, then cut into fingers and remove from the tin. Store in an airtight container.

Quick and Easy Teabread

This succulent, fruity teabread can be served just as it is, or spread with a little butter. The loaf can be stored, tightly wrapped in foil or in an airtight container, for up to five days. A great way to get children to eat some fruit, this teabread is ideal for packed lunches, picnics, or simply served with a cup of tea for afternoon tea.

SERVES EIGHT

350g/12oz/2 cups luxury mixed dried fruit

75g/3oz/scant ⅓ cup demerara (raw) sugar, plus 15ml/1 tbsp

1 large (US extra large) egg

175g/6oz/1½ cups self-raising (self-rising) flour

1 Put the fruit in a bowl. Add 150ml/¼ pint/⅔ cup boiling water and leave to stand for 30 minutes.

2 Preheat the oven to 180°C/350°F/Gas 4. Grease and line the base and long sides of a 450g/1lb loaf tin (pan).

3 Beat the main quantity of sugar and the egg into the fruit. Sift the flour into the bowl and stir until combined. Turn into the prepared tin and level the surface. Sprinkle with the remaining sugar.

4 Bake the teabread for about 50 minutes, until risen and firm to the touch. When the bread is cooked, a skewer inserted into the centre will come out without any sticky mixture on it. Leave the loaf in the tin for 10 minutes before turning out on to a wire rack to cool.

Scottish Morning Rolls

These soft, spongy bread rolls are irresistible while still warm and aromatic. Made with milk, rather than the more usual water, they have a rich flavour. In Scotland they are a firm favourite for breakfast but they are also great served for tea, spread with thick butter and rich fruit jam. To speed up the rising time, place the rolls in the airing cupboard or on the top of the preheated oven.

MAKES TEN ROLLS

450g/1lb/4 cups unbleached strong white bread flour, plus extra for dusting

10ml/2 tsp salt

20g/¾oz fresh yeast

150ml/¼ pint/⅔ cup lukewarm milk, plus extra for glazing

1 Grease two baking sheets. Sift the flour and salt together into a large bowl and make a well in the centre. Mix the yeast with the milk, then mix in 150ml/¼ pint/⅔ cup lukewarm water. Add to the centre of the flour and mix together to form a soft dough.

2 Knead the dough lightly in the bowl, then cover with lightly oiled clear film (plastic wrap) and leave to rise in a warm place for 1 hour, or until doubled in bulk. Turn the dough out on to a lightly floured surface and knock back (punch down).

3 Divide the dough into ten equal pieces. Knead lightly and, using a rolling pin, shape each piece of dough into a flat oval 10 x 7.5cm/ 4 x 3in, or a flat round 9cm/3½in.

4 Transfer to the prepared baking sheets, spaced well apart, and cover the rolls with oiled clear film. Leave to rise, in a warm place, for about 30 minutes.

5 Meanwhile, preheat the oven to 200°C/400°F/Gas 6. Press each roll in the centre with the three middle fingers to equalize the air bubbles and to help prevent blistering. Brush with milk and dust with flour. Bake for 15–20 minutes, or until lightly browned. Dust with more flour and cool slightly on a wire rack. Serve warm.

Split Loaf

Freshly baked white bread makes a really simple, yet utterly delicious, tea-time snack. Cut the warm bread into thick slices and spread with homemade fruit jam.

MAKES ONE LOAF

500g/1¼lb/5 cups unbleached strong white bread flour, plus extra for dusting

10ml/2 tsp salt

15g/½oz fresh yeast

60ml/4 tbsp lukewarm milk

1 Grease a 900g/2lb loaf tin (pan). Sift the flour and salt into a bowl and make a well in the centre. Mix the yeast with 150ml/¼ pint/⅔ cup lukewarm water. Stir in another 150ml/¼ pint/⅔ cup lukewarm water. Pour the yeast mixture into the centre of the flour and using your fingers, mix in a little flour to form a smooth batter.

2 Sprinkle a little more flour from around the edge over the batter and leave in a warm place for about 20 minutes to "sponge". Add the milk and remaining flour; mix to a firm dough.

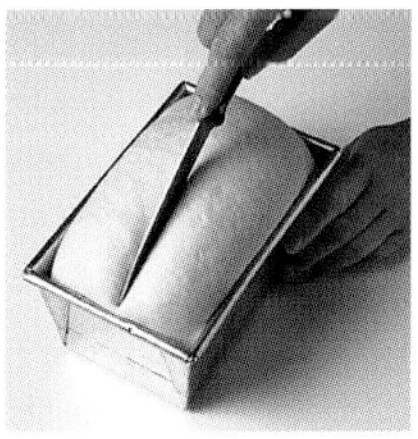

3 Place on a lightly floured surface and knead for about 10 minutes, until smooth and elastic. Place in a lightly oiled bowl, cover with lightly oiled clear film (plastic wrap) and leave to rise in a warm place for 1–1¼ hours, or until nearly doubled in bulk.

4 Knock back (punch down) the dough and turn out on to a lightly floured surface. Shape it into a rectangle, the length of the prepared tin. Roll the dough up lengthways, tuck the ends under and place, seam side down, in the tin. Cover the loaf and leave to rise in a warm place for about 20–30 minutes.

5 Using a sharp knife, make one deep central slash. Dust the top of the loaf with a little sieved flour. Leave for 10–15 minutes. Meanwhile, preheat the oven to 230°C/450°F/Gas 8. Bake for 15 minutes, then reduce the oven temperature to 200°C/400°F/Gas 6. Bake for 20–25 minutes, until golden when it sounds hollow when tapped on the base. Cool on a wire rack.

Strawberry Jam

This is the classic fragrant preserve for English afternoon tea, served with freshly baked scones and clotted cream. It is also extremely good stirred into plain yogurt for breakfast. When choosing strawberries for making jam, pick undamaged, slightly underripe fruit if possible – the pectin content will be high and ensure a good set.

1kg/2¼lb/8 cups small strawberries

900g/2lb/4 cups granulated sugar

juice of 2 lemons

MAKES ABOUT 1.3KG/3LB

1 Layer the strawberries and sugar in a large bowl. Cover and leave overnight.

2 The next day, scrape the strawberries and their juice into a large, heavy pan. Add the lemon juice. Gradually bring to the boil over a low heat, stirring until the sugar has dissolved.

3 Boil steadily for 10–15 minutes, or until the jam registers 105°C/220°F on a sugar thermometer. Alternatively, test for setting by spooning a small amount on to a chilled saucer. Chill for 3 minutes, then push the jam with your finger: if wrinkles form on the surface, it is ready. Cool for 10 minutes.

4 Stir the jam before pouring it into warm sterilized jars, filling them right to the top. Cover with waxed paper discs immediately, but do not seal with lids until the jam is completely cold.

COOK'S TIP

For best results when making jam, don't wash the strawberries unless absolutely necessary. Instead, brush off any dirt, or wipe the strawberries with a damp cloth. If you have to wash any, pat them dry and then spread them out on a clean dishtowel to dry.

Bramble Jelly

The tart, fruity flavour of wild blackberries makes this jelly one of the tastiest, especially for serving with hot buttered toast, English muffins or warm scones. It has to be made with hand-picked wild blackberries for the best flavour. Make sure you include a small proportion of red unripe berries for a good set.

MAKES 900G/2LB

900g/2lb/ 8 cups blackberries

juice of 1 lemon

about 900g/2lb/ 4 cups caster (superfine) sugar

1 Put the blackberries and lemon juice into a large pan (use a preserving pan with two handles if possible). Add 300ml/½ pint/1¼ cups water. Cover the pan and cook for 15–30 minutes, or until the blackberries are very soft.

2 Ladle into a jelly bag or a large sieve (strainer) lined with muslin (cheesecloth) and set over a large mixing bowl. Leave the fruit to drip overnight to obtain the maximum amount of juice. Do not disturb or squeeze the bag or the jelly will be cloudy.

3 Discard the fruit pulp. Measure the juice and allow 450g/1lb/2 cups sugar to every 600ml/1 pint/2½ cups juice. Place the juice and sugar in a large, heavy pan and bring to the boil, stirring constantly until the sugar has dissolved.

4 Boil the mixture rapidly until the jelly registers 105°C/220°F on a sugar thermometer, or test for setting by spooning a small amount on to a chilled saucer (keep a saucer in the freezer for this purpose). Chill for 3 minutes, then push the mixture with your finger: if wrinkles form on the surface of the jelly, it is ready.

5 Skim off any scum and immediately pour the jelly into warm sterilized jars. Cover and seal immediately, then label when the jars are cold.

Desserts

THERE'S NOTHING BETTER AFTER A DELICIOUS MAIN MEAL THAN A SUMPTUOUS DESSERT – BUT OFTEN IT CAN SEEM LIKE TOO MUCH EFFORT. THIS CHAPTER OFFERS UP THE PERFECT ANSWER WITH A WHOLE COLLECTION OF MOUTHWATERING DESSERTS. FROM POACHED FRUIT TO BAKED CUSTARDS AND RICH AND INDULGENT ICE-CREAMS, YOU ARE SURE TO FIND THE PERFECT SWEET TREAT IN THIS CHAPTER.

Papayas in Jasmine Flower Syrup

The fragrant syrup can be prepared in advance, using fresh jasmine flowers from a house plant or the garden. You can also use fresh flowers as a garnish. The syrup tastes fabulous with papayas, but it is also good with all sorts of desserts. Try it with ice cream or spooned over lychees or mangoes.

SERVES FOUR

45ml/3 tbsp palm sugar or light muscovado (brown) sugar

20–30 jasmine flowers

2 ripe papayas

juice of 1 lime

1 Place 105ml/7 tbsp water in a small pan and add the sugar. Heat gently, stirring occasionally, until the sugar has dissolved, then simmer, without stirring, over a low heat for 4 minutes.

2 Pour into a bowl, leave to cool slightly, then add the jasmine flowers. Leave to steep for at least 20 minutes.

3 Peel the papayas and slice in half lengthways. Scoop out and discard the seeds. Place the papayas on serving plates and squeeze over the lime.

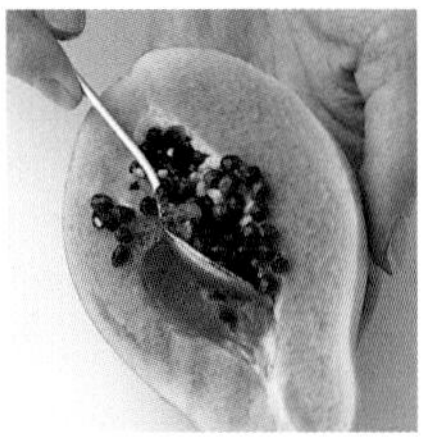

4 Strain the syrup into a clean bowl, discarding the flowers. Spoon the syrup over the papayas. If you like, decorate with a few fresh jasmine flowers.

Mango and Lime Fool

Canned mangoes are used here for convenience, but this zesty, tropical fruit fool tastes even better if made with fresh ones. Choose a variety with a good flavour, such as the fragrant Alphonso mango.

SERVES FOUR

400g/14oz can sliced mango, plus extra to garnish (optional)

grated rind of 1 lime, plus juice of ½ lime

150ml/¼ pint/⅔ cup double (heavy) cream

90ml/6 tbsp Greek (US strained plain) yogurt

1 Drain the canned mango slices and put them in a food processor, then add the grated lime rind and lime juice. Process until the mixture forms a smooth purée.

2 Alternatively, place the mango slices in a bowl and mash with a potato masher, then press through a sieve (strainer) into a bowl with the back of a wooden spoon. Stir in the lime rind and juice.

3 Pour the cream into a bowl and add the yogurt. Whisk until the mixture is thick and then quickly whisk in the mango mixture.

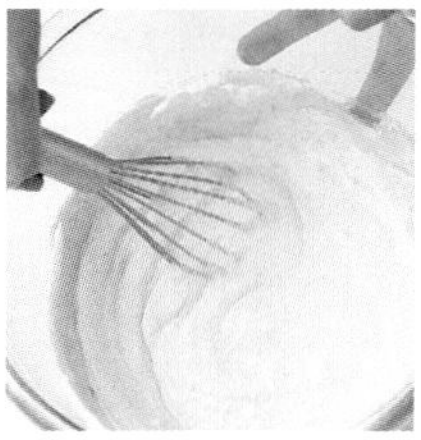

4 Spoon the fool into four tall cups or glasses and chill for at least 1 hour. Just before serving, decorate each glass with fresh mango slices, if you like.

Juniper-scented Pears in Red Wine

More often used in savoury dishes than sweet, juniper berries have a dark blue, almost black colour with a distinct gin-like flavour. In this fruity winter dessert crushed juniper berries give the classic partnership of pears and red wine a slightly aromatic flavour. These pears are particularly good sprinkled with toasted almonds and whipped cream.

SERVES FOUR

30ml/2 tbsp juniper berries

50g/2oz/¼ cup caster (superfine) sugar

600ml/1 pint/2½ cups red wine

4 large or 8 small firm pears, stalks intact

1 Lightly crush the juniper berries using a pestle and mortar or with the end of a rolling pin. Put the berries in a pan with the sugar and wine and heat gently until the sugar dissolves.

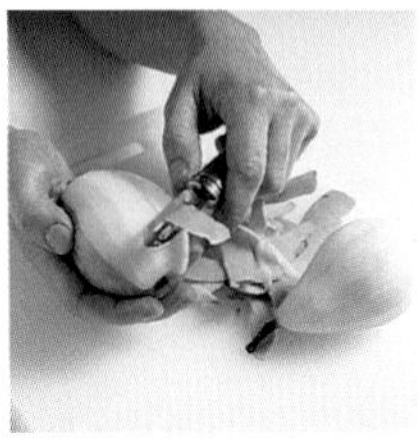

2 Meanwhile, peel the pears, leaving them whole. Add them to the wine and heat until just simmering. Cover the pan and cook gently for about 25 minutes, until the pears are tender. Turn the pears once or twice to make sure they cook evenly.

3 Use a slotted spoon to remove the pears. Boil the syrup hard for a few minutes, until it is slightly reduced and thickened. If serving the pears hot, reheat them gently in the syrup, otherwise arrange them in a serving dish and spoon the syrup over.

Rhubarb and Ginger Jellies

Made with bright pink, young rhubarb, these softly set jellies get the taste buds tingling. They are spiced with plenty of fresh ginger, which gives just a hint of zesty warmth. Pour the jelly into pretty glasses and serve it as it is or top it with spoonfuls of lightly whipped cream.

SERVES FIVE TO SIX

1kg/2¼lb young rhubarb

200g/7oz/1 cup caster (superfine) sugar

50g/2oz fresh root ginger, finely chopped

15ml/1 tbsp powdered gelatine

1 Cut the rhubarb into 2cm/¾in chunks and place in a pan with the sugar and ginger. Pour in 450ml/¾ pint/scant 2 cups water and bring to the boil. Reduce the heat, cover and simmer gently for 10 minutes, until the rhubarb is very soft and pulpy.

2 Meanwhile, sprinkle the gelatine over 30ml/2 tbsp cold water in a small heatproof bowl. Leave to stand, without stirring, for 5 minutes, until the gelatine has become sponge-like in texture. Set the bowl over a small pan of hot water and simmer, stirring occasionally, until the gelatine has dissolved completely into a clear liquid. Remove from the heat.

3 Strain the cooked rhubarb through a fine sieve (strainer) into a bowl. Stir in the dissolved gelatine until thoroughly mixed. Leave to cool slightly before pouring into serving glasses. Chill for at least 4 hours or overnight, until set.

Oranges in Syrup

This recipe works well with most citrus fruits – for example, try pink grapefruit or sweet, perfumed clementines, which have been peeled but left whole. Serve the oranges with 300ml/½ pint/1¼ cups whipped cream flavoured with 5ml/1 tsp ground cinnamon, or 5ml/1 tsp ground nutmeg or with Greek (US strained plain) yogurt.

SERVES SIX

6 medium oranges

200g/7oz/1 cup sugar

100ml/3½fl oz/ scant ½ cup fresh strong brewed coffee

50g/2oz/½ cup pistachio nuts, chopped (optional)

COOK'S TIP *Choose a pan in which the oranges will just fit in a single layer – use a deep frying pan if you don't have a pan that is large enough.*

1 Finely pare, shred and reserve the rind from one orange. Peel the remaining oranges. Cut each one crossways into slices, then re-form them, with a cocktail stick (toothpick) through the centre.

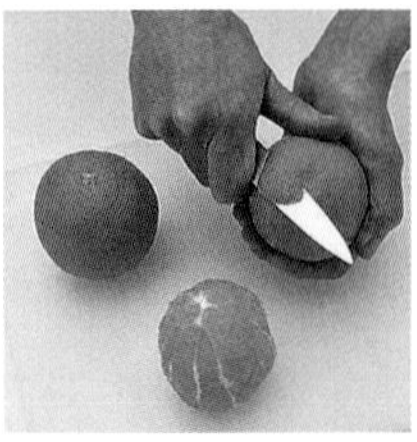

2 Put the sugar in a heavy pan and add 50ml/2fl oz/¼ cup water. Heat gently until the sugar dissolves, then bring to the boil and cook until the syrup turns pale gold.

3 Remove from the heat and carefully pour 100ml/3½fl oz/ scant ½ cup freshly boiling water into the pan. Return to the heat until the syrup has dissolved in the water. Stir in the coffee.

4 Add the oranges and the rind to the coffee syrup. Simmer for 15–20 minutes, turning the oranges once during cooking. Leave to cool, then chill. Serve sprinkled with pistachio nuts, if using.

Fresh Fig Compote

A vanilla and coffee syrup brings out the wonderful flavour of figs – serve Greek (US strained plain) yogurt or vanilla ice cream with the poached fruit. A good selection of different honey is available – its aroma and flavour will be subtly scented by the plants surrounding the hives. Orange blossom honey works particularly well in this recipe, although any clear variety is suitable.

SERVES FOUR TO SIX

400ml/14fl oz/ 1⅔ cups fresh brewed coffee

115g/4oz/½ cup clear honey

1 vanilla pod (bean)

12 slightly under-ripe fresh figs

1 Choose a frying pan with a lid, large enough to hold the figs in a single layer. Pour in the coffee and add the honey.

2 Split the vanilla pod lengthways and scrape the seeds into the pan. Add the vanilla pod, then bring to a rapid boil and cook until reduced to about 175ml/6fl oz/¾ cup.

3 Wash the figs and pierce the skins several times with a sharp skewer. Cut in half and add to the syrup. Reduce the heat, cover and simmer for 5 minutes. Remove the figs from the syrup with a slotted spoon and set aside to cool.

4 Strain the syrup over the figs. Allow to stand at room temperature for 1 hour before serving.

COOK'S TIP *Figs come in three main varieties – red, white and black – and all three are suitable for cooking. They are sweet and succulent, and complement the stronger, more pervasive flavours of coffee and vanilla very well.*

Coconut Custard

This delicious, creamy dessert can be baked or steamed and is great served with fresh fruit. Mangoes go particularly well. Serve dusted with icing (confectioners') sugar and garnished with mint leaves.

SERVES FOUR

4 eggs

75g/3oz/6 tbsp soft light brown sugar

250ml/8fl oz/1 cup coconut milk

5ml/1 tsp vanilla, rose or jasmine extract

1 Preheat the oven to 150°C/300°F/Gas 2. Whisk the eggs and sugar in a bowl until smooth, then add the coconut milk and vanilla, rose or jasmine extract and whisk well.

2 Strain the mixture into a jug (pitcher), then pour it into four individual heatproof glasses, ramekins or an ovenproof dish.

3 Stand the glasses, ramekins or dish in a roasting pan. Fill the pan with hot water to reach halfway up the sides of the ramekins or dish. Bake for 35–40 minutes, or until the custards are set. Test with a fine skewer or cocktail stick (toothpick).

4 Remove the roasting pan from the oven, lift out the ramekins or dish and leave to cool before serving. If you like, turn out the custards on to serving plate(s).

Baked Thai-style Rice Pudding

Black glutinous rice, also known as black sticky rice, has long dark grains and a nutty taste reminiscent of wild rice. This baked pudding is a classic Thai dessert and has a distinct character and flavour.

SERVES FOUR TO SIX

175g/6oz/1 cup black or white glutinous rice

60ml/4 tbsp sugar

475ml/16fl oz/2 cups coconut milk

3 eggs

1 Combine the rice and half the sugar in a pan. Pour in half the coconut milk and 250ml/8fl oz/1 cup cold water. Bring to the boil, reduce the heat to low and simmer, stirring occasionally, for about 20 minutes, or until the rice has absorbed most of the liquid. Preheat the oven to 150°C/300°F/Gas 2.

2 Spoon the rice mixture into a large ovenproof dish or divide it among individual ramekins. Beat the eggs with the remaining coconut milk and sugar, then pour over the rice.

3 Place the dish or ramekins in a roasting pan and pour in enough hot water to come halfway up the sides of the dish or ramekins. Cover with foil and bake for 35–60 minutes, or until the custard has set. Serve warm or cold.

Peach and Cardamom Yogurt Ice

Make the most of spices that are familiar in savoury cooking by discovering their potential for sweet dishes. Cardamom, often used in Indian cooking, has a warm pungent aroma and a subtle lemon flavour. Although it is made with yogurt rather than cream, this ice cream has a luxurious velvety texture, and it is a healthy choice, too.

SERVES FOUR

8 cardamom pods

6 peaches, total weight about 500g/1¼lb, halved and stoned (pitted)

75g/3oz/6 tbsp caster (superfine) sugar

200ml/7fl oz/scant 1 cup natural (plain) yogurt

1 Put the cardamom pods on a board and crush them with the base of a ramekin, or place in a mortar and crush with a pestle.

2 Chop the peaches coarsely and put them in a pan. Add the crushed cardamom pods, with their black seeds, the sugar and 30ml/2 tbsp water. Cover and simmer for 10 minutes, or until the fruit is tender. Leave to cool.

3 Process the peach mixture in a food processor or blender until smooth, then press through a sieve (strainer) placed over a bowl.

4 Mix the yogurt into the sieved purée and pour into a freezerproof container. Freeze for 5–6 hours, until firm, beating once or twice with a fork, electric whisk, or in a processor to break up the ice crystals.

5 Scoop the ice cream on to a large platter and serve.

Blackberry Ice Cream

There could scarcely be fewer ingredients in this delicious, vibrant ice cream, which is simple to make and ideal as a prepare-ahead dessert. Serve the ice cream with biscuits (cookies), such as shortbread or almond biscuits, to provide a delicious contrast in taste and texture.

SERVES FOUR TO SIX

500g/1¼lb/5 cups blackberries, hulled, plus extra to decorate

75g/3oz/6 tbsp caster (superfine) sugar

300ml/½ pint/1¼ cups whipping cream

crisp dessert biscuits (cookies), to serve

COOK'S TIP

Frozen blackberries can be used instead of fresh. You will need to increase the cooking time to 10 minutes and stir occasionally.

1 Put the blackberries into a pan, add 30ml/2 tbsp water and the sugar. Cover and simmer for 5 minutes, until just soft.

2 Tip the fruit into a sieve (strainer) placed over a bowl and press it through the mesh, using a wooden spoon. Leave to cool, then chill.

3 Whip the cream until it is just thick but still soft enough to fall from a spoon, then mix it with the chilled fruit purée. Pour the mixture into a freezerproof container and freeze for 2 hours, or until it is part frozen.

4 Mash the mixture with a fork or process it in a food processor to break up the ice crystals. Return it to the freezer for 4 hours more, mashing or processing the mixture again after 2 hours.

5 Scoop the ice cream into dishes and decorate with extra blackberries. Serve with crisp dessert biscuits.

Coconut Ice

The creamy taste and texture of this ice cream comes from the natural fat content of coconut, as the mixture contains neither cream nor egg and is very refreshing. The lime adds a delicious tangy flavour as well as pretty green specks to the finished ice. Decorate with toasted coconut shavings or toasted desiccated (dry unsweetened shredded) coconut (this browns very quickly, so watch it constantly).

SERVES FOUR TO SIX

115g/4oz/generous ½ cup caster (superfine) sugar

2 limes

400ml/14fl oz can coconut milk

toasted coconut shavings, to decorate (optional)

COOK'S TIP

To make toasted coconut shavings, rinse the flesh from a coconut under cold water. Shave slices using a vegetable peeler, then toast under a moderate grill (broiler) until they are curled and the edges have turned golden.

1 Pour 150ml/¼ pint/⅔ cup water in a small pan. Tip in the caster sugar and bring to the boil, stirring constantly until the sugar has completely dissolved. Remove the pan from the heat and leave the syrup to cool, then chill well.

2 Grate the rind from the limes finely, taking care to avoid the bitter pith. Squeeze out their juice and add to the pan of syrup with the rind. Add the coconut milk.

3 Pour the mixture into a freezerproof container and freeze for 5–6 hours, or until firm. Beat twice with a fork or electric whisk, or process in a food processor to break up the crystals. Scoop into dishes and decorate with toasted coconut shavings, if you like.

Gingered Semi-freddo

This Italian ice cream is rather like the original soft scoop ice cream. Made with a boiled sugar syrup rather than a traditional egg custard, and generously speckled with chopped stem ginger, this delicious ice cream will stay soft when frozen. For a really impressive dinner party dessert, serve the semi-freddo in plain (semisweet) chocolate cases.

SERVES SIX

1 Mix the sugar and 120ml/4fl oz/½ cup cold water in a pan and heat gently, stirring occasionally, until the sugar has dissolved.

2 Increase the heat and boil for 4–5 minutes, without stirring, until the syrup registers 119°C/238°F on a sugar thermometer. Alternatively, test by dropping a little of the syrup into a cup of cold water. Pour the water away and you should be able to mould the syrup into a small ball.

3 Put the egg yolks in a large heatproof bowl and whisk until frothy. Place the bowl over a pan of simmering water and whisk in the sugar syrup. Continue whisking until the mixture is very thick. Remove from the heat and whisk until cool.

4 Whip the cream and lightly fold it into the egg yolk mixture with the chopped stem ginger. Pour into a freezerproof container and freeze for 1 hour.

5 Stir the semi-freddo to bring any ginger that has sunk to the base of the container to the top, then return it to the freezer for 5–6 hours, until firm. Scoop into dishes or chocolate cases (*see* Cook's Tip). Decorate with slices of ginger and serve.

115g/4oz/generous ½ cup caster (superfine) sugar

4 egg yolks

300ml/½ pint/1¼ cups double (heavy) cream

115g/4oz/⅔ cup drained stem (preserved) ginger, finely chopped, plus extra slices, to decorate

COOK'S TIP

To make the cases, pour melted chocolate over squares of baking parchment and drape them over upturned glasses. Peel off the baking parchment when set.

Nutritional Information

The nutritional analysis below is per portion, unless otherwise stated.

p18 Simple Cream of Onion Soup
Energy 499kcal/2073kJ; Protein 4g; Carbohydrate 21g, of which sugars 15g; Fat 45g, of which saturates 28g; Cholesterol 118mg; Calcium 89mg; Fibre 3.5g; Sodium 0.6 g.

p19 Potato and Roasted Garlic Broth
Energy 122kcal/515 kJ; Protein 5g; Carbohydrate 25g, of which sugars 1g; Fat 1g, of which saturates 0g; Cholesterol 0mg; Calcium 12mg; Fibre 2.2g; Sodium 0.9g.

p20 Winter Squash Soup with Tomato Salsa
Energy 255kcal/1059kJ; Protein 3g; Carbohydrate 18g, of which sugars 12g; Fat 19g; of which saturates 3g; Cholesterol 0mg; Calcium 86mg; Fibre 3.1g; Sodium 0.1g.

p21 Vichyssoise
Energy 186kcal/781kJ; Protein 5g; Carbohydrate 16g,of which sugars 4g; Fat 4g, of which saturates 2g; Cholesterol 17mg; Calcium 8mg; Fibre 0.1g; Sodium 0.1g.

p22 Sweet and Salty Vegetable Crisps
Energy 64kcal/265kJ; Protein 1g; Carbohydrate 3g,of which sugars 3g; Fat 0g, of which saturates 1g; Cholesterol 0mg; Calcium 8mg; Fibre 0.7g; Sodium 0.1g.

p23 Sizzling Prawns
Energy 109kcal/450kJ; Protein 2g; Carbohydrate 1g,of which sugars 0g; Fat 11g, of which saturates 2g; Cholesterol 17mg; Calcium 8mg; Fibre 0.1g; Sodium 0.1g.

p24 Yogurt Cheese in Olive Oil
Energy 1927kcal/7943kJ; Protein 32g; Carbohydrate 10g,of which sugars 10g; Fat 201g, of which saturates 47g; Cholesterol 0mg; Calcium 758mg; Fibre 0.0g; Sodium 0.4g.

p25 Baked Eggs with Creamy Leeks
Energy 219kcal/905kJ; Protein 9g; Carbohydrate 2g, of which sugars 2g; Fat 19g, of which saturates 10g; Cholesterol 261mg; Calcium 61g; Fibre 1.2g; Sodium 0.1g.

p26 Potato and Onion Tortilla
Energy 512kcal/2132kJ; Protein 15g; Carbohydrate 40g, of which sugars 5g; Fat 34g, of which saturates 6g; Cholesterol 285mg; Calcium 73mg; Fibre 3.7g; Sodium 0.1g.

p27 Red Onion and Goat's Cheese Pastries
Energy 554kcal/2308kJ; Protein 13g; Carbohydrate 48g, of which sugars 8g; Fat 36g, of which saturates 6g; Cholesterol 27mg; Calcium 128mg; Fibre 1.6g; Sodium 0.5g.

p28 Pepperonata
Energy 140kcal/583kJ; Protein 2g; Carbohydrate 8g, of which sugars 8g; Fat 11g, of which saturates 2g; Cholesterol 0mg; Calcium 19mg; Fibre 2.0g; Sodium 0.1g.

p28 Artichoke and Cumin Dip
Energy 37kcal/155kJ; Protein 2g; Carbohydrate 2g, of which sugars 1g; Fat 3g, of which saturates 0g; Cholesterol 0mg; Calcium 29mg; Fibre 0.1g; Sodium 0.1g.

p32 Spaghettini with Roasted Garlic
Energy 637kcal/2670kJ; Protein 14g; Carbohydrate 77g, of which sugars 4g; Fat 33g, of which saturates 5g; Cholesterol 2mg; Calcium 53mg; Fibre 3.1g; Sodium 0.1g.

p33 Spaghetti with Raw Tomato and Ricotta Sauce
Energy 530kcal/2230kJ; Protein 14g; Carbohydrate 69g, of which sugars 7g; Fat 24g, of which saturates 5g; Cholesterol 14mg; Calcium 100mg; Fibre 3.8g; Sodium 0.1g.

p34 Rosemary Risotto with Borlotti Beans
Energy 362kcal/1517 kJ; Protein 11g; Carbohydrate 38g, of which sugars 4g; Fat 20g, of which saturates 8g; Cholesterol 19mg; Calcium 80mg; Fibre 65g; Sodium 0.9 g.

p35 Mussel Risotto
Energy 348kcal/459kJ; Protein 15g; Carbohydrate 31g, of which sugars 4g; Fat 19g, of which saturates 7g; Cholesterol 351mg; Calcium 83mg; Fibre 6.5g; Sodium 0.7g.

p36 Spiced Lentils
Energy 326kcal/1372kJ; Protein 24g; Carbohydrate 34g, of which sugars 4g; Fat 11g, of which saturates 7g; Cholesterol 35mg; Calcium 235mg; Fibre 6.2g, Sodium 0.8g.

p37 Jansson's Temptation
Energy 688kcal/2859 kJ; Protein 15g; Carbohydrate 51g, of which sugars 1g; Fat 49g, of which saturates 29g; Cholesterol 134mg; Calcium 182mg; Fibre 4.6g; Sodium1.0 g.

p38 Baked Salmon with Caraway Seeds
Energy 665kcal/2758kJ; Protein 51g; Carbohydrate 0g, of which sugars 0g; Fat 34g, of which saturates 20g; Cholesterol 186mg; Calcium 61mg; Fibre 0g; Sodium 0.3g.

p39 Tonno con Piselli
Energy 329kcal/1379kJ; Protein 30g; Carbohydrate 23g, of which sugars 8g; Fat 14g, of which saturates 4g; Cholesterol 40mg; Calcium 83mg; Fibre 6.8g; Sodium 0.6g.

p40 Sea Bass in a Salt Crust
Energy 200kcal/842 kJ; Protein 39g; Carbohydrate 0g, of which sugars 0g; Fat 5g, of which saturates 1g; Cholesterol 160mg; Calcium 261mg; Fibre 0g; Sodium 2.2g.

p41 Fish with Tomato and Pine Nuts
Energy 308 kcal/1294kJ; Protein 42g; Carbohydrate 6g, of which sugars 3g; Fat 13g, of which saturates 2g; Cholesterol 80mg; Calcium 94mg; Fibre 1.0g; Sodium 0.4g.

p42 Drunken Chicken
Energy 343kcal/1437kJ; Protein 39g; Carbohydrate 1g, of which sugars 1g; Fat 11g, of which saturates 3g; Cholesterol 158mg; Calcium 38mg; Fibre 0.1g; Sodium 0.1g.

p43 Turkey Patties
Energy 155kcal/651kJ; Protein 26g; Carbohydrate 1g, of which sugars 1g; Fat 5g, of which saturates 1g; Cholesterol 79mg; Calcium 11mg; Fibre 0.1g; Sodium 0.1 g.

p44 North African Lamb
Energy 412kcal/1716 kJ; Protein 34g; Carbohydrate 16g, of which sugars 14g; Fat 24g, of which saturates 11g; Cholesterol 127mg; Calcium 36mg; Fibre 2.7g; Sodium 0.2g.

p45 Lamb Steaks with Redcurrant Glaze
Energy 301kcal/1258kJ; Protein 24g; Carbohydrate 12g, of which sugars 12g; Fat 17g, of which saturates 8g; Cholesterol 94mg; Calcium 10mg; Fibre 0.0g; Sodium 0.1g.

p46 Beef Patties with Onions and Peppers
Energy 339kcal/1416 kJ; Protein 30g; Carbohydrate 15g, of which sugars 11g; Fat 18g, of which saturates 6g; Cholesterol 70mg; Calcium 60mg; Fibre 4.0g; Sodium 0.1g.

p47 Steak with Tomato Salsa
Energy 175kcal/736kJ; Protein 25g; Carbohydrate 3g, of which sugars 7g; Fat 3g, of which saturates 69g; Cholesterol 69mg; Calcium 18mg; Fibre 0.9g; Sodium 0.1g.

p50 Anchovy and Roasted Pepper Salad
Energy 86kcal/366kJ; Protein 6g; Carbohydrate 12g, of which sugars 11g; Fat 2g, of which saturates 0g; Cholesterol 8mg; Calcium 57mg; Fibre 4.0g; Sodium 0.5g.

p51 Potato and Olive Salad
Energy 296kcal/1246kJ; Protein 5g; Carbohydrate 48g, of which sugars 4g; Fat 11g, of which saturates 2g; Cholesterol 0mg; Calcium 40mg; Fibre 3.3g; Sodium 0.3g.

p52 Globe Artichokes with Green Beans and Garlic Dressing
Energy 371kcal/1528kJ; Protein 4g; Carbohydrate 5g, of which sugars 3g; Fat 38g, of which saturates 6g; Cholesterol 0mg; Calcium 60mg; Fibre 1.2g; Sodium 0.1g.

p53 Asparagus with Lemon Sauce
Energy 84kcal/349kJ; Protein 6g; Carbohydrate 7g, of which sugars 4g; Fat 3g, of which saturates 1g; Cholesterol 90mg; Calcium 58mg; Fibre 2.9g; Sodium 0.1g.

p54 Minty Broad Beans with Lemon
Energy 118kcal/493kJ; Protein 7g; Carbohydrate 9g, of which sugars 2g; Fat 7g, of which saturates 1g; Cholesterol 0mg; Calcium 35mg; Fibre 69g; Sodium 0.1g.

p54 Gingered Carrot Salad
Energy 82kcal/339kJ; Protein 1g; Carbohydrate 7g, of which sugars 7g; Fat 7g, of which saturates 1g; Cholesterol 0mg; Calcium 70mg; Fibre 2.1g; Sodium 0.1g.

p56 Baked Winter Squash
Energy 139kcal/583kJ; Protein 4g; Carbohydrate 12g, of which sugars 10g; Fat 9g, of which saturates 1g; Cholesterol 0mg; Calcium 98mg; Fibre 3.9g; Sodium 0.1 g.

p57 Stewed Okra with Tomatoes and Coriander
Energy 79kcal/332 kJ; Protein 7g; Carbohydrate 9g, of which sugars 8g; Fat 2g, of which saturates 1g; Cholesterol 0mg; Calcium 355mg; Fibre 8.7g; Sodium 0.1 g.

p58 Tomato and Aubergine Gratin
Energy 229 kcal/952 kJ; Protein 6g; Carbohydrate 6g, of which sugars 6g; Fat 20g, of which saturates 5g; Cholesterol 9mg; Calcium 125mg; Fibre 40g; Sodium 0.1g.

p59 Baked Leek and Potato Gratin
Energy 574 kcal/2394 kJ; Protein 20g; Carbohydrate 43g, of which sugars 5g; Fat 37g, of which saturates 23g; Cholesterol 108mg; Calcium 257mg; Fibre 4.6g; Sodium 0.3g.

p60 Fennel, Potato and Garlic Mash
Energy 374kcal/1560 kJ; Protein 7g; Carbohydrate 38g, of which sugars 4g; Fat 23g, of which saturates 6g; Cholesterol 17mg; Calcium 73mg; Fibre 6.2g; Sodium 0.1g.

p61 Bubble and Squeak
Energy 205kcal/854 kJ; Protein 3g; Carbohydrate 23g, of which sugars 4g; Fat 12g, of which saturates 1g; Cholesterol 0mg; Calcium 30mg; Fibre 2.8g; Sodium 0.1 g.

p62 Tandoori Rotis
Energy 218kcal/922kJ; Protein 7g; Carbohydrate 37g, of which sugars 1g; Fat 5g, of which saturates 3g; Cholesterol 11mg; Calcium 23mg; Fibre 5.3g; Sodium 0.4g.

p63 Yemeni Sponge Flat Breads
Energy 393kcal/1660kJ; Protein 9g; Carbohydrate 68g, of which sugars 1g; Fat 11g, of which saturates 7g; Cholesterol 27mg; Calcium 126mg; Fibre 2.7g; Sodium 0.6g.

p66 Creamed Coconut Macaroons
Energy 83kcal/344kJ; Protein 1g; Carbohydrate 6g, of which sugars 6g; Fat 10g, of which saturates 5g; Cholesterol 29mg; Calcium 7mg; Fibre 0.6g; Sodium 0.1g.

p67 Almond Cookies
Energy 94kcal/394kJ; Protein 1g; Carbohydrate 12g, of which sugars 8g; Fat 5g, of which saturates 3g; Cholesterol 11mg;Calcium 13mg; Fibre 0.3g; Sodium 0.1g.

p68 Golden Ginger Macaroons
Energy 59kcal/248kJ; Protein 2g; Carbohydrate 5g, of which sugars 5g; Fat 4g, of which saturates 0g; Cholesterol 13mg; Calcium 20mg; Fibre 0.5g; Sodium 0.1g.

p68 Nutty Nougat
Energy 2251kcal/9514kJ; Protein 28g; Carbohydrate 416g, of which sugars 413g; Fat 64g, of which saturates 5g; Cholesterol 312mg;Calcium 25mg; Fibre 0.8g; Sodium 0.1g

p70 All Butter Cookies
Energy 99kcal/419kJ; Protein 1g; Carbohydrate 11g, of which sugars 3g; Fat 6g, of which saturates 4g; Cholesterol 16mg; Calcium 15mg; Fibre 0.3g; Sodium 0.1 g.

p71 Almond Cigars
Energy 171kcal/721kJ; Protein 4g; Carbohydrate 28g, of which sugars 22g; Fat 5g, of which saturates 1g; Cholesterol 29mg; Calcium 25mg; Fibre 0.8g; Sodium 0.1 g.

p72 Rich Chocolate Biscuit Slice
Energy 408kcal/1711kJ; Protein 3g; Carbohydrate 36g, of which sugars 30g; Fat 29g, of which saturates 18g; Cholesterol 44mg; Calcium 55mg; Fibre 1.1g; Sodium 0.1 g.

p73 Orange and Pecan Scones
Energy 192kcal/806kJ; Protein 3g; Carbohydrate 18g, of which sugars 1g; Fat 12g, of which saturates 3g; Cholesterol 12mg; Calcium 87mg; Fibre 1.2g; Sodium 0.1 g.

p74 Chewy Flapjacks
Energy 276kcal/1038kJ; Protein 3g; Carbohydrate 29g, of which sugars 14g; Fat 14g, of which saturates 8g; Cholesterol 34mg; Calcium 16mg; Fibre 1.4g; Sodium 0.1g.

p75 Quick and Easy Teabread
Energy 239kcal/1017kJ; Protein 4g; Carbohydrate 56g, of which sugars 40g; Fat 1g, of which saturates 0g; Cholesterol 32mg; Calcium 116mg; Fibre 1.6g: Sodium 0.6 g.

p76 Scottish Morning Rolls
Energy 165kcal/701kJ; Protein 6g; Carbohydrate 35g, of which sugars 1g; Fat 1g, of which saturates 0g; Cholesterol 2mg; Calcium 2mg; Fibre 1.4g; Sodium 0.2g.

p77 Split Loaf
Energy 1770kcal/7527kJ; Protein 65g; Carbohydrate 380g, of which sugars 10g; Fat 10g, of which saturates 3g; Cholesterol 8mg; Calcium 784mg; Fibre 15.5g; Sodium 4.0g.

p78 Strawberry Jam (per 15ml/1 tbsp)
Energy 42kcal/161kJ:Protein 0g; Carbohydrate 11g, of which sugars 11g; Fat 0g, of which saturates 0g; Cholesterol 0mg; Calcium 3mg; Fibre 0.1g; Sodium 0g.

p79 Bramble Jelly (per 15ml/ 1 tbsp)
Energy 63kcal/268kJ:Protein 0g; Carbohydrate 17g, of which sugars 17g; Fat 0g, of which saturates 0g; Cholesterol 0mg; Calcium 8mg; Fibre 0.0g; Sodium 0g.

p82 Papayas in Jasmine Flower Syrup
Energy 251kcal/1057kJ; Protein 1g; Carbohydrate 38g, of which sugars 38g; Fat 0g, of which saturates 0g; Cholesterol 0mg; Calcium 39mg; Fibre 5.5g; Sodium 0.1g.

p83 Mango and Lime Fool
Energy 289kcal/1204kJ; Protein 2g; Carbohydrate 21g, of which sugars 21g; Fat 22g, of which saturates 14g; Cholesterol 51mg; Calcium 62mg; Fibre 0.7g; Sodium 0g.

p84 Juniper Scented Pears in Red Wine
Energy 251kcal/1057kJ; Protein 1g; Carbohydrate 38g, of which sugars 38g; Fat 0g, of which saturates 0g; Cholesterol 0mg; Calcium 39mg; Fibre 5.5g; Sodium 0.1g.

p85 Rhubarb and Ginger Jellies
Energy 179kcal/765kJ; Protein 2g; Carbohydrate 45g, of which sugars 44g; Fat 0g, of which saturates 0g; Cholesterol 0mg; Calcium 193mg; Fibre 2.8g; Sodium 0.1g.

p86 Oranges in Syrup
Energy 236kcal/1001kJ; Protein 3g; Carbohydrate 48g, of which sugars 48g; Fat 5g, of which saturates 1g; Cholesterol 0mg; Calcium 82mg; Fibre 3.0g; Sodium 0.1g.

p86 Fresh Fig Compote
Energy 156kcal/667kJ; Protein 2g; Carbohydrate 38g, of which sugars 38g; Fat 0g, of which saturates 0g; Cholesterol 0mg; Calcium 67mg; Fibre 2.5g; Sodium 0.1g.

p88 Coconut Custard
Energy 177kcal/748kJ; Protein 8g; Carbohydrate 23g, of which sugars 23g; Fat 7g, of which saturates 2g; Cholesterol 232mg; Calcium 60mg; Fibre 0g; Sodium 0.2g.

p89 Baked Thai-style Rice Pudding
Energy 310kcal/1302kJ; Protein 10g; Carbohydrate 52g, of which sugars 22g; Fat 6g, of which saturates 2g; Cholesterol 174mg; Calcium 70mg; Fibre 0g; Sodium 0.2g.

p90 Peach and Cardamom Yogurt Ice
Energy 155kcal/659kJ; Protein 4g; Carbohydrate 33g, of which sugars 33g; Fat 2g, of which saturates 0g; Cholesterol 1mg; Calcium 126mg; Fibre 1.9g; Sodium 0.1g.

p91 Blackberry Ice Cream
Energy 391kcal/1621kJ; Protein 3g; Carbohydrate 28g, of which sugars 28g; Fat 30g, of which saturates 19g; Cholesterol 79mg; Calcium 97mg; Fibre 3.9g; Sodium 0.1g.

p92 Coconut Ice
Energy 137kcal/583kJ; Protein 0g; Carbohydrate 35g, of which sugars 35g; Fat 0g, of which saturates 0g; Cholesterol 0mg; Calcium 33mg; Fibre 0.0g; Sodium 0.1 g.

p93 Gingered Semi-freddo
Energy 397kcal/1694kJ; Protein 3g; Carbohydrate 29g, of which sugars 28g; Fat 31g, of which saturates 18g; Cholesterol 203mg; Calcium 45mg; Fibre 0g; Sodium 0.1g.

Index